Ink Pen Diva: The Truth Behind my Pen

By: Tamika L. Sims

Foreword by: J Haleem

www.inkpendiva.com

ISBN: 978-8-218-06083-1

This book may be purchased in bulk for promotional, educational, or business use. Contact Publisher by e-mail: info@jhaleem.com.

CONTENTS

DEDICATION

To the aspiring entrepreneur whose story is yet to be written, may you find encouragement and hope on these pages.

ACKNOWLEDGEMENTS

It feels weird and exciting all at the same time to be writing again. That said, there are a few people I wish to acknowledge.

First, I thank my Heavenly Father for the gift & the grace of writing. Thank you for the words that flow through my veins and into the hearts of those who need them.

To my mom, thank you for the gift of life, your constant encouragement, and prayers. No matter what, I know I always you in my corner.

To my son, I am grateful that God chose me to be your mother. You are one of my life's greatest gifts.

To my sister, my Trixie, I love you. You have always believed in me and my gift. I wait in great anticipation for the creation of *Tamika's Song*.

To my nephews, Jameer & Ja'len, I absolutely love being an Auntie, more importantly yours.

To my Ace in the hole, Jay, there are not enough words for me to say thank you. My life changed when I met you. Thank you for being one of the kindest and most selfless individuals I know.

To Emerald, Sydney Jo, & JJ, thank you for accepting me and all of my crazy.

To everyone who has contributed in any way to not only my

entrepreneurial journey, but the book of *Tamika*, I appreciate you.

To the more than 200 of you that have chosen me to help birth your book baby – I pray nothing but the greatest of successes and richest of God's blessings over your life.

EPIGRAPH

========================
========================

"There will come a time when you believe everything is finished. That will be the beginning."

Louis L' Amour

============================
============================

FOREWORD

Usually, you don't get the opportunity to speak to somebody for a whole hour uninterrupted when you first meet them. It's a blessing when you do get that opportunity because you get to learn so much about the other person, you get to see and know what makes them tick, what they like, and what their interests are. You get to see if you guys' mesh.

A lot of times when you meet people, you might be at an outing or have others around. Because of this, you are not able to get that much time. But my first-time meeting Tamika, I was able to talk to her for more than an hour with no interruption. I learned how much we had in common, how much we enjoyed entertainment and current events, and us being able to talk about pretty much anything.

What I didn't know is that there was another side to her. I didn't know that she was going through a whole lot of turmoil. I didn't know that she was fighting to get herself out of a situation. I soon realized that she was making some adjustments and changes to her brand. She talked with me extensively about helping her make those adjustments because at the time that's what I did. The one thing that stuck out to me the most because I didn't like it was that she wanted to change the name of her business.

At the time she called herself the *Ink Pen Diva* and I liked that name. I thought that it was super cool, especially since we were going to be working together on my project as well. However, she wanted to have a classier name. She wanted to appeal to a bigger and better audience. She wanted to call her company, *Get Write With Tamika* and I couldn't convince her otherwise. Get Write With Tamika was born. Us working closely together and getting to know her more, I learned more about her struggles and the other things that she was dealing with.

I started to see her resilience. I started to see more and more of her greatness. I started to see more and more of her skillset. She wouldn't have called it that or been able to identify it as that. But I recognized it being of kindred spirit, being the person who came from those same issues, those same traumas, and not having much family support. And when it comes to business, feeling alone, and being in a situation of not knowing where you are going to stay and not knowing how you are going to feed yourself.

I immediately understood exactly what she was going through, but me being in a mature state in my life, I understood the greatness in that as well. I was seeing her handle business, not only with me, but handle business with people in different parts of the country and making sure that they're able to do what they need to do. She was able to help them tell their stories and actually guide people through some of the roughest parts of their lives.

It's not easy telling your story. It's not easy writing the book and dealing with the emotions that come from writing the book. It's not easy to navigate that space. I wouldn't recommend nobody do it alone, but to be able to help people in that space and through those ordeals while you're carrying a weight on your shoulder, it's definitely not helping people to *get write*. You're actually living a lifestyle.

I wanted to tell her that. And I kept telling her that through this process of helping me and me watching her help everybody else, I said, *"You're not helping people get write."* I said, *"You're being a diva.*

And that just means that you're living a lifestyle in which nobody can take your power away from you. No matter what you're doing, no matter what you're going through, you're showing strength, and walking in your purpose."

It doesn't matter what it looks like today. You're doing the things you're supposed to be doing. Life is cyclical. And your time is going to come back around. As long as you are walking in your purpose, keeping your head up and doing the things God has called you to do, you are going to be in position to take advantage of the opportunity when it comes back around to you.

To be standing here, or I guess sitting here, in this full circle moment of Tamika's and being able to watch with the bird's eye view; and sometimes with a magnifying glass, seeing her come from not only helping other people get right, but watching her get right and not only become the woman that she wanted to be, but become even more than she ever thought that she could be.

She now understands. I think that you guys are going to understand that she is not only walking in her purpose as a diva, but she truly understands what it means to be a diva. She's choosing with this book and going forward to be the Ink Pen Diva.

I'm truly excited about what's going to come from this project, but I'm even more excited that I had a chance to be right there with her during the process. I pray that you guys enjoy this book as much as I did.

God bless,

J Haleem, CPC

Three-Time Author & Motivational Speaker

Principle, J Haleem, LLC

INTRODUCTION

iden·ti·ty
the condition of being the same
with something described or
asserted

It's been 11 years since I have released anything remotely close to a journey or story about my life. Sure, I've written a total of five books since the release of my debut novel, *The Plus Factor,* but none produced have been like the book you are reading today. I have my reasons and as you continue reading throughout the various chapters, I'm hoping you will understand why it has taken me so long. As you will be able to see, some of this time has been good and some of it has been bad.

Truth be told, I did *not* want to write this book. I shied away from writing this book. I didn't think I had another book in me. Once I created my business, I became focused more on pushing and promoting my clients and helping them publish their stories. Eventually, I took on the incredible task of Ghostwriting a project. And I am happy I did. That project reawakened my gift of writing. It awakened my creativity in a way that had not been explored in quite some time. And, ultimately, it is why you are reading this book.

When I first began this process, I had no idea that you would be holding the finished product you have before you. Revision after revision, edit after edit, all a part of the necessary process, none of which I regret. The creative process can be so messy, but I love it.

And now here I am. Back in the saddle. Ready to give to you what has been given to me. My journey. My story. Given to you without the self-imposed limits. I'm breaking out of the box I placed myself in. And I'm not piecing it together anymore. This time, I'm giving you the entire story because it deserves to be told.

So, here goes.

Ink Pen Diva was the name of my literary business when I first began my career. Eventually, it became my moniker. The thing I was known for. Ink pen, for the proverbial ink pen many writers use to craft their stories. That is if they are an old-fashioned writer like me who still enjoys pen and paper. And diva, well because you know...I can at times be a *little* ... extra. Don't laugh. This was my baby born out of a time in my life, where I had lost my identity. And I'm so happy to report that I have found it again and this time, I plan on holding on to her.

I hope you'll get as much out of reading it as I have creating it. I hope you learn something, not only about me but also about yourselves. You see, I believe we all have a story. Thank you for sharing this space with me.

Our time starts now.

Cheers

~ XX Tamika

CHAPTER ONE

What's in Your Entrepreneurial Garden?

I first met Tamara Canzater, creator of Woman to Woman Entrepreneur Association in 2013 on Facebook. Woman to Woman, originally named WOW, was a membership association for women business leaders in Columbia, SC. Tamara hosted monthly empowerment brunches that featured time for networking, great conversation, and an empowerment speaker.

The speaker was always the highlight or drawing card for the event. I was still relatively new to the speaking arena from this perspective and at this point, I had no desire or thought to start a business. However, I appreciated the camaraderie, and I enjoyed being in the company of women who were doing good work in my local community.

At this point, I had only been published for approximately two years and was becoming comfortable with the fact that I was now an author and wrapping my head around the idea of my story forever being inked for generations. I hired a publicist approximately one year after releasing my book and through our working together, I had had my first professional photo shoot, which led to the creation of my first media or press kit.

The press kit was the first of my deliverables from her company. We needed this to have to send to the local television and radio stations, she was pitching me to, and it was a great addition to my arsenal. Each opportunity to appear as a guest on a local radio or television station gave me the time to share my expertise on domestic and sexual violence. I am a survivor and have always been a free giver of my story.

Because my debut novel was about my experience as a domestic violence survivor -this was the topic of the bulk of my speaking engagements. Right around the time that I started working with her, I began a new job as a Quality Data Specialist for a local hospital system. I have always likened this to my first 'grown-up' job. My first real *professional* job after getting my degree.

I graduated with my bachelor's degree in Information Technology from South University - Columbia campus and although I loved my job working for Sistercare, Inc. a local nonprofit agency that serves domestic violence victims, it was no longer enough financially to care for my responsibilities as a homeowner and as a mom. I was committed to the mission, but I also had to be practical.

The funny story behind this is I almost missed the opportunity to get this job. After submitting my application, it wasn't long before I received the call from Human Resources. After my first interview, I had two more, both of which were group interviews. That position served as support staff for the education and quality outcomes wing of the hospital and because of this, I had to meet with staff from both areas of the department I was interviewing with.

I mentioned before that I got my degree in Information Technology, but you never heard me say I had any medical knowledge. When I applied for this job, I did so strictly on my skills, educational background, and the fact that I am a pretty quick learner. There wasn't anything I couldn't do well if shown the way.

After the third round of interviews, my manager and director at the time decided they were going to hire me and the HR

Generalist, Joel, went on the hunt to try and find me. He had been trying to reach me and wasn't able to. I didn't know this because, for some reason I changed my cell phone number. He finally decided to call my place of employment and on his third attempt, he was able to reach me and offered me the job that came with a salary increase of more than $10,000. I was extremely apologetic and thanked him for his diligence. I guess the third time's the charm.

Because I had no medical knowledge, I had a serious learning curve - not only the one that comes with learning a new office culture and work environment but in my case, with this position - there was also medical knowledge. I knew nothing about wound care, ostomy, nursing indicators, or how much of a role fecal matter can play in our health. Yes - ladies and gentlemen - there is such a thing as fecal transplants.

However, there was a guardian angel waiting for me, and her name was Bree. I'll never forget her. She was so committed to my success in this position that in addition to her daily work responsibilities, she told my boss that if they were willing to hire me, she would take me under her wing and personally train me.

Although the staff was quite interested in me, they were hesitant because I had no medical background or healthcare experience. And yet Bree was willing to take a chance, she saw something in me. Even to the point of buying me a medical dictionary.

The dictionary would give me basic medical knowledge to help me have even the simplest of conversations and understand exactly *what* I was doing every day. This was a big help to me. I studied this book day and night. It was almost as if I was a college student again, studying as if my life depended on it. I will always appreciate Bree's gesture. Switching from a predominant non-profit industry career to the medical field was a big change. And I don't know if I would have made it in that job if she hadn't taken on that responsibility.

While I was enjoying my employment at the hospital, something else was starting to happen. I started receiving inquiries from aspiring authors who had already written their books, but they couldn't find anyone to edit. They knew I had written a book, so they asked me. These requests began to trickle in and slowly over time, they increased. Again, nothing had entered my mind about starting a business, I saw it as me helping these authors out. I don't even remember charging. I have always had a love and passion for writing and reading, so this was right up my alley.

The requests would become more frequent, and I knew then because of the time I was investing, I had to ask for something. I think the most I ever asked for at that time was $50.

And then I received a message on Facebook one day from Tamara. She stated that she had been watching my growth and wondered whether or not I would be interested in serving as the next guest speaker for Woman to Woman? I was both flattered by the gesture and also taken aback. Based on what I knew about Woman-to-Woman, and the networking brunches I had participated in, every speaker had been an entrepreneur or was pursuing some sort of entrepreneurial journey. I was not. I reminded her that I did not have a business, nor any desire to start one, I was only helping some folks edit their books whenever I was asked.

She heard what I was saying but would not take no for an answer. I finally gave in. She gave me her original topic, which was *Planting the Seed.* We couldn't quite pull this together and after a bit of back and forth, I suggested another topic, *What's in Your Entrepreneurial Garden?*

Having no knowledge about entrepreneurship, this was the best I could do at the time and gardening seemed to be a good topic for women. I thought well, hey, let's give it a shot. Let's try. I was always good with research, so that would be my approach. I would research the topic of entrepreneurship and present it in a way that would be helpful, engaging, and insightful.

She and I talked often over the next couple of weeks to make sure I had everything and for her to review any final details with me. The day finally came, and it was time for me to speak. This was November and I remember it being very chilly. Walking into the door, I didn't know this presentation would forever change my life. I remember being such an inexperienced speaker that I only walked in with my presentation. I didn't even have enough sense or wherewithal to bring any books with me. I can even recall what I was wearing on that day - an orange shirt, dark blue jeans, a black leather jacket, and heels.

I was a confident speaker, every job I had required me to do public speaking or some interfacing with the community in some capacity. However, what brought on additional nervousness was the fact that I was presenting on *entrepreneurship*.

I walked around the room as I typically do, even now, and shook hands and introduced myself to those I hadn't met or seen before. On this particular day, there were women there from all over the state of South Carolina. One woman was a recent transplant from Los Angeles.

After Tamara introduced me, I stepped into the spotlight - so to speak. It was time for me to shine and share what I had prepared. Throughout the time that I was speaking, I could see those Aha moments on the faces of the women, a few head nods coupled with their smiles - this fed my energy and helped to ease the nervousness I was still experiencing even after I began talking.

Once the presentation was over, there was time for a brief Q&A period, approximately 10-15 minutes. Right at about 7.5 minutes in, a woman named Ebony raised her hand. Ebony was a local web designer and she and I had met prior to. It was Ebony's question that planted the seed. She asked in that open forum why I wasn't speaking on writing a book?

I immediately responded and told her because I didn't know how to teach someone about writing a book and that I had only written one and it was only one year old at this point. She understood, but what happened next was truly a blessing from God. The women in the room all started to verbally express their desire to tell their story one day.

I kind of stepped back and watched for a minute as this sentiment echoed around the room. Finally, I spoke up and asked, "If I were to offer a course teaching you how to write a book, who would be interested?" Every woman in that room raised her hand. I was shocked. I think I even asked the question, only expecting a minimal response. I don't think I said much after that, there wasn't much else to say. The seed had been planted. Now it was time for me to water it.

CHAPTER TWO

Taking the Top Off

After leaving the women's entrepreneurship brunch, I got in the car with my mom. She needed to use my car that Saturday morning, so I had her drop me off, this way she could complete her errands. When I got in the car with her, she asked me how the speaking engagement went? After pausing for a minute, I told her that it went a little differently than I expected.

She asked me to explain, and I went on to say that those ladies, every one of them, had expressed an interest in writing a book. The only difference is that this is not what I was invited to speak on. Because of this I was not prepared, with anything to offer them. My mom smiled with a glow only a mother could have as they sit back filled with pride and utter amazement when their child does something good. She encouraged me in that moment and did what she always does, which is tell me to pray about it. I told her I would, and we proceeded to drive out of the parking lot.

The rest of the day was a blur. I don't remember anything else about that afternoon, except doing what my mother suggested and that was going to God in prayer. First, I asked Him if it was His will for me to create something for writers and if it were, I asked Him to guide me on my next steps. I knew this next move would be pivotal and I wanted to be sure that I was doing what was best.

I am not sure how God answers your prayers, but when I pray about something specific and am really intentional and strategic in my prayers, going to God with a specific ask - He answers. This has occurred multiple times in my life. I'm even specifically remembering a time with my son's father - but I digress. Just know. He sees. He hears. He cares. LOL.

Within a few days, I received my answer. I'm a writer, so I tend to have a notebook with me. Over the next couple of days, whenever I would receive a download, I immediately jot it down and went to work. The first thing I did was research businesses in Columbia, SC, that help writers. I wasn't even sure what a person who helped people write books was called. I tapped into the only resource I had back then to find my answer, Google.

The first thing I researched was the answer to the question of if there was someone or a company already providing this type of service. I've not ever been the type to create something that someone was already doing, so I wanted to see what was out there. I was able to find through my search that these individuals were called writing coaches and that there were writing coaches or writing services offered in the world of academia, for master's Level Thesis or Doctoral Dissertations. I wasn't interested in that area, so seeing that did not alter my thought process of exactly who I wanted to serve and how I wanted to serve them.

What I did discover is that this was an open lane - especially with helping writers creatively through fiction, non-fiction, and self-help books. In addition to the ladies in that room of the women's networking brunch, seeing that there was space and opportunity for me to provide this service in my local area, solidified it for me.

From there, I immediately went to work. I started getting some things down on paper, well, on the computer, so this picture in my mind, could start coming together. The only thing that stumped me, is that I was unsure of what to name it. As a result, I started asking myself questions such as, is this a business or only a service that I will offer? Do I create something for groups or individuals?

One day out of the blue or so it seemed to me, I was scrolling Instagram. This wasn't anything unusual, and at the time, I only had maybe 100 followers. I must have created a post about writing and not too long after that, I saw the bubble notification pop up, indicating that someone left a comment. The comment asked a very simple question, only it wouldn't be by the time this exchange happened.

My follower asked, "How is my ink pen diva today?" Now, usually, when someone leaves a comment on my social media, I'm a fast responder. You can call me *Jane on the Spot!* This time I paused. I kept repeating: Ink pen diva. Ink pen diva. Over and over again. And honey, that was it! *That's it!* I said to myself, the name of my service would be *Ink Pen Diva*.

At that moment, everything became clear. Not only did I now have a name for what would become my business, but I knew how I would serve them. I decided that I would launch a 10-week group coaching for writers' program, with the overall goal of helping individuals become better writers. Since this was my first time ever launching a service, I didn't want to start with books. After all, I had only written one and except for the advice and thoughts of a couple of friends, I was completely on my own. Quite frankly, I didn't feel confident in my ability to teach anyone what I barely knew how to do.

Now that I had a name for it, I wanted to have a logo designed. I reached out to one of the people I consider to be one of the best in the game - Tamara with *Finkbeiner Design Firm*. I was first introduced to Tamara through my church, Rhema Christian Center COGIC, located in West Columbia. Any and all graphic design created for the church, she was behind it. And in my opinion, she never failed. When the time came for her to design my logo, I knew she would do the same.

Now, full disclosure - I am NOT creative visually, my creativity is with words. I don't design. I don't know what colors match up well with other colors. I knew nothing about brand boards or Mood Boards. So, when I approached Tamara, I led with this. Here is the name of my service, this is what I'm doing, have at it. I didn't know the color scheme I wanted, or font choices. When I say I had nothing, I had nothing. I told her to do her thing and I was sure I would be happy with it.

And happy I was! I IMMEDIATELY loved it! I even think I screamed a little bit. Who am I kidding? I let out a loud scream when I opened the *Gmail* notification. It was perfect. It was a great combination of creativity and structure. That's how I saw myself. That's how I still see myself, especially as I have grown through the years.

It was all starting to come together. I had a business name. I had a logo. I had a pretty decent outline. I would even have them sign a *Writer's Contract*. And I would do it all for $350. This was totally bad. Monetarily, I was making $35/person a week for 10-weeks and that was really me being overconfident thinking if I could sell out, my first time out of the gate.

Next, came logistics. I would need a flyer designed so that I could have to distribute to fill these seats. I reached out to Ascension Marketing Co and spoke with them about creating a flyer that would serve a dual purpose, not only for advertising, but also as the cover for the Handbook that each participant would receive. Let's say that graphic design wise, I looked very good in the digital streets.

Next, I started thinking about how I wanted to deliver my weekly sessions. I knew that I wanted each session recorded, so, the next thing I would do is look for renting space in a commercial recording studio. I connected with a local Gospel musician who taught piano, who had a studio she owned for her students to come and practice their weekly lessons.

I had known her for some time and the beautiful blessing in this is that she didn't charge me at all to use the studio for the one hour I would need to record the lesson. At this point, I had everything I thought I needed to get started. Now, it was time to go full swing into promoting.

In all of the getting and purchasing I was doing; I didn't once think of getting a website designed or creating a business Facebook page. If you're a gambling person, then you may be able to surmise that I relied on my personal social media to fill this program. I shared, shared, shared. Hoping to catch the attention of someone, anyone who had a desire to become a better writer.

Well, as they say hard work pays off, but it would be months before I would ever see the fruit.

CHAPTER THREE

Daddy

My relationship with my father was great when I was growing up. He was attentive, the smartest man I knew (even though he only had an eighth-grade education), and never missed anything, *anything* that pertained to my sister's and my education. From the outside looking in he was great - but on the inside, he had a drug habit that would show its ugly head in our household many, many nights.

As I got older, our relationship became strained. The drugs

became his family, and he stayed close to its members. Whether pill, snorting, or smoking, nothing could ever keep him away from his children for extended periods of time. He always showed up and even if he wasn't living with us, he called on the day of every report card release to make sure we were staying on point. He continued this even when we became mothers. Education was important to him, and we knew it.

I know you may be wondering why am I telling you this? It's because I want you to understand that as much as this book is about my entrepreneurship journey it also about yours, and the answer is that I can't tell my origin story without talking about him. Right about the time that I spoke at the Woman to Woman Women's

Entrepreneurship Brunch, I received a letter from my father. I had moved into a townhouse recently and we were still getting settled in. My sister and nephews were living with me at the time.

I thought him writing us a letter was unusual because my dad had not ever done this before. It was a simple note, handwritten. I remember the words were at a slant. The letter stated that he had been diagnosed with cancer and the doctors had only given him seven months to live. He said he would try to come see us. He was going to catch a bus and come before it was too late.

This brought me to tears because I could not imagine continuing on the rest of my life without knowing that my dad was not going to be here. Even though our relationship was strained as an adult, I still didn't ever think about burying either of my parents. I tried to keep going on with putting together the business plan, but my world was rocked approximately two weeks later.

My uncle called my sister to deliver the news. Before we got that call from my uncle, I had actually taken the opportunity to write my dad a letter. I responded to the letter that he had sent to my sister and me. In the letter, I said to him that I was sorry to hear about his diagnosis, but that he would be okay, and we looked forward to seeing him in the Summer. I told him not to worry about my sister and I because our Heavenly Father would be here to take care of us. He would never know my final thoughts. He passed away before he ever received that letter.

We were at home for the evening. I was sitting at the dining room table and my sister was in the kitchen making lamb chops. She answered the phone, but all I could hear her saying was, "What?" "Slow down." "I can't understand you." She was trying to make sense of what my uncle was saying on the phone because clearly, he was distraught. And at this point I didn't know what was going on. I only remember looking at her.

When she finally hung up the phone, she said, "he's gone." "Whose, gone?" I asked. "Daddy..." she said, "He's gone." My uncle had walked home in the afternoon and found him sitting on the couch. My uncle said something to him and assumed he was sleeping when he didn't answer him. He kept calling his name, hoping to wake him. Once he walked over and touched him, he realized then - he had already peacefully passed away.

Immediately, the tears filled my eyes. All I could think is that he didn't get my letter. He never got the chance to read my final thoughts. He didn't read my words and see that I loved him. He passed away not knowing this. I'm sure he knew we loved him as his children. I only wished for and wanted one more moment to say that to him or be able to pick up the phone or do any of those things. Unfortunately, I was not granted that wish. I had to reconcile with the death of my father, that God told him in his own way that we would be okay.

And he found comfort and peace in that.

My father had been in a lot of pain prior to him receiving his cancer diagnosis. His health had already started deteriorating. He had recently moved with my uncle to Missouri, and they were doing his best to provide him with the best medical care. The doctors had to run a series of tests They originally found the cancer on his pancreas, and it spread to his liver. Once it spread to another vital organ, his death happened in a matter of days. Both cancers are aggressive, and death can happen quickly. In the midst of launching my company and starting my business, I had to bury my father.

For most people, if they weren't mentally strong in any way that would've been devastating. And I imagine most folks would've either put their business on hold or stopped doing it all together, seeing this as some sign that they should not continue. But I knew that that would never be what my father would want. He was proud of us and the accomplishments that he was able to see, we were able to make before he passed away.

He saw me get my degree and was one month shy of seeing my sister receive her degree. He was there for our children being born. In those moments, he was able to express love and be proud of us until he was no longer on this side. Because my father was living in Missouri at the time, planning his funeral was a completely different process than one would traditionally think. Some of which was working with the Coroner's office in Missouri, airlines, and then securing a funeral service back home in Columbia, SC to handle transport. Of course, I had just started a business. My sister was working, but she had recently had my nephew and our money was tight. It was difficult for us to even get up the money, to pay for the funeral. My grandfather was still living at the time, (he has since passed away); but he was able to help us offset some of the cost by paying for a portion of it.

He was in his early nineties and his health would not allow him to make the service, so this was his contribution. We were truly grateful for it. With his donation, we were able to pay a deposit to the funeral home and make payment arrangements on the balance, so that we could move the process forward. My father passed away in February and we were able to have his service early April.

This was an extremely difficult time for me, being a new business owner and also dealing with the death of a parent that has been hard and it still continues to be hard to this day. Losing a parent is a significant loss and there is a permanent hole that's always going to be there, but I am grateful for God. My Heavenly Father, who still continues to give me that fatherly guidance and wisdom. And from time-to-time, I am thankful that even that I even get to still hear my father's voice or have him show up in one of my dreams.

Special Note:

Daddy, I never wrote a public acknowledgement to you in my debut novel, *The Plus Factor*, but I hope that as you rest eternally, you rest with the knowledge somehow that your "Miki," is honoring your memory.

CHAPTER FOUR

Half of a Woman

When I launched Ink Pen Diva in 2014, I told you guys that it started off pretty slow. Relatively low money was made during that first year in business. And of course, after dealing with the death of my father, I really had to recommit myself. I know that sounds crazy since that was so close to the beginning, but that was heartbreaking. Try as I might, it was difficult to bounce back from that. However, bounce back I did.

2015 started off better, but it wouldn't end that way. Following the year after my dad's death, we had to deal with Probate Court because my father didn't leave a will, and there were some bank accounts, a payout from a city bus accident, and his financial matters in the state of Missouri that needed our attention.

This took the next year or so to get completely worked out. Once all of his legal matters were fully resolved, I could fully commit myself to working on my business. Not making a lot of money when I first started out in business was This not a problem because I still maintained my full-time job. I always had income coming in, which meant that I could continue to keep myself afloat, still take care of my household expenses, and participate in anything else I desired.

At the beginning of March, I became seriously ill. Initially, I thought it was a stomach bug because of the symptoms I was experiencing. Nausea. Vomiting. Loose bowels. I remember calling off for work, deciding I would take it easy, eat some broth, and Ginger Ale and be back to work the next day. Throughout the day, I became progressively worse.

Now, the vomiting and loose bowels became full-blown diarrhea and at this point, I couldn't hold anything down, not even water. Then the pain began. Once the evening hit, the pain intensified to a 9/10 and I could no longer stand. I remember laying in my living room floor and saying to myself that this was not a stomach bug, something was wrong.

I laid down for a little bit longer and finally asked my sister to take me to the local Urgent Care. I needed to be seen and be seen fast. At this point, I was walking with a limp, damn near in tears. My sister parked the car and met me inside of the lobby. My name was called about 15 minutes later.

The Doctor on duty completed the normal routine of taking my temperature, height/weight, blood pressure, and then asked my symptoms. He had a nurse to draw some blood. He left the room and came back several minutes later. He asked me, what I thought was a very silly question. "Could you be pregnant?" I immediately said, "No. I haven't missed a period or anything." He said, "Well, you are and I'm afraid it's why you're so sick. The fetus is not viable."

He then proceeded to ask the name of my gynecologist so that he could give him a call. He called Dr. Estes and explained the situation as well as to find out what the next course of action should be. Dr. Estes wanted me to go to the ER and from there, the gynecologist on duty could give him a more accurate assessment of what was happening.

I finished up at Urgent Care and drove to the closest ER, which happened to be at the location I worked. I checked in. They checked my vitals and took some other precautions for blood clots because I have a family history of them. It was confirmed that I was in fact experiencing an ectopic pregnancy and I would need to have emergency surgery.

I was sent back home for the evening but had an appointment first thing in the morning with Dr. Estes. When I arrived at his office, his nurse took more vitals and then I had to have an ultrasound. The fetus was in fact six weeks and had a heartbeat. This part of the appointment sucked; I would have rather not seen that.

At the same time that this was happening, paperwork and phone calls were made to prepare for this emergency surgery. From his office, I was walked to the Pre-Op Department, so that I could get ready for my procedure. I kept my boss informed this entire time and by the time I made it to Pre-Op, I called to let her know I was there and she and one of my co-workers came and sat with me.

My sister was with me and needed to go back and make some arrangements for my nephew. However, when thc time came for me to be moved to the OR Waiting Room, she had come back to the hospital. He was able to talk with both of us, let us know that he didn't anticipate any problems and that he would be removing the fetus along with my right ovary and fallopian tube. The surgery was expected to last about one hour.

Of course, I don't remember anything about the operation, I was placed under general anesthesia. However, once I was placed in the PACU, Dr. Estes explained to me that I experienced a minor complication during the surgery that caused me to hemorrhage. He was able to control and eventually stop the bleeding and finish the operation.

I didn't stay in the PACU long. This was an outpatient surgery, and I would be going home within the hour. I wasn't sure what to expect from a recovery perspective because I had never had any type of surgery before. Outside of the flu and an acute sinus infection, I had never been ill. The first few days were rough, I needed help to stand and shower because I was still a minor fall risk.

I was able to take advantage of the Short-Term Disability available through the hospital's healthcare plan, to assist with the lost wages. I had my post op appointment a couple of weeks later. I was given all clear to return to work. Only this time with half of my reproductive system.

I dealt with thoughts & feelings of being less than a woman. I was still in my thirties, and I still had a desire to have another child. A daughter specifically. Immediately, thoughts began to hit my mind of thinking it would never happen for me. I know many other women have felt this way and can relate to these feelings I had. For some women, they would go on to bear other children. Unfortunately, physically birthing another baby was not in the clouds for me. At the time that this book is being written, I get to care for not just one, but two children and I am perfectly happy and perfectly at peace.

CHAPTER FIVE

The Prayer that Changed it All

At the beginning of 2016, I began experiencing a complete influx of new clients. I'd been in business for a couple of years at this point, but I was now moving past the coaching space of helping people to become better writers. I was now moving more into the space of actually helping people put books together. Once I fully released that as a service and took the plunge into book coaching, that is when business turned around.

January to September of 2016, my client roster stayed full. At one point, I had a waiting list of individuals waiting to get into my program. I sold out my program during the course of those nine months and the money that I was able to bring in through Ink Pen Diva was well over what I was making at the hospital, so much so, that I did not have to touch my paychecks. I was able to save while building, generating a nice "nest egg," for myself. I can't remember how much I was able to save, but it was in the thousands.

September 2016, I started thinking seriously about my business and wondering if this was something that I could do full-time. I'll never forget going to God in prayer one day, asking Him for guidance for the next steps in my business and what direction I should take. The reason I started doing this, besides needing to pray was because you know how you're on your job, but you also have a business and you find yourself doing your business on your job, the one that you're actually getting paid to do? Yes, that was me. LOL.

I almost got caught by my manager and director a couple of times. I can laugh about this now, but it certainly was not funny back then. I was sitting at my desk, and I said to myself that something has to give. I cannot continue to do both concurrently and have the same level of success in both places. I had a great job, and I didn't want to lose it. However, I didn't want to not continue to show up in my business. I started praying and once again I asked God a set of specific questions.

"God, what will you have me to do next? What is my next step? Should I take the plunge and move into full-time entrepreneurship? Should I continue to work this business as a side hustle until I can continue to save up more money?"

I will tell you guys something. I don't know about your relationship with God. I don't know if you believe in God or any sort of higher power that exists in the universe. And this is not a religious book at all.

However, as it pertains to my relationship with God, He answers me, especially when I am intentional about my prayers and specific with my request and needs, as you guys saw with the launch of the business. After I finished praying, I immediately heard March 31st, 2017. Once I heard the date, I knew that March 31st would be my last day working as an employee.

Once I got the date, I started to share with people that I knew in the business space, particularly business coaches. There responses were, *"Oh no! You need to keep working. You need to keep saving and building up your money."*

I heard them out. I listened to their thoughts and opinions. After all, these were people I respected. Otherwie, I would've never asked. On the other hand, I also know what I heard, and I know what I felt in my spirit. I knew that if I would've remained at that job a little bit longer, I would've been disobedient to what I felt God was leading me to do, stepping into full-time entrepreneurship.

The other thing that happened is I started questioning God and asked if, He was sure? Isn't it funny how we question the One we pray to for answers? No matter how many times I prayed and asked God for reassurance, I kept getting the same answer, March 31st, 2017. For the next six months, from September to March 1st, which is when I would submit my resignation, I worked hard.

I worked hard to continue to serve my clients at the optimum level because I knew that as I served them, they would serve as my ambassadors and refer their friends & family to me. They would send people to me that they knew were interested in writing a book. At this point, my writing coaching program had significantly grown, and it was amazing.

In the process of working hard, I also continued to save and build. I did this until February 26th. This is the date I typed my resignation letter to hand deliver it to my boss. My job at the time required that any one in my position give a 30-day notice, versus the traditional two-weeks that most folks are used to.

I had no problem giving them the 30-day notice, that would work out for me in the long run. Two additional paychecks to save prior to fully taking the plunge. Besides, it was a good job that I had, and I wanted to leave it properly. Working at the hospital, did a lot for me, especially as far as being able to utilize my degree.

In 2011, I graduated from South University with my degree in Information Technology. Before I worked at the hospital, I worked for a great nonprofit, but nonprofits, at least the one that I worked for, did not have technology budgets. With my degree, at the hospital, I was able to create and implement systems that were still in use when I left in 2017.

March 1st came, and I remember it being on a Monday. Mondays were significant to my boss and me. It was the day that we decided to have our weekly meeting, where she and I would do check-ins. I would get the schedule for the week, let her know what I was currently working on, and if she needed my assistance with any special projects. And then the next Monday, we would share any updates that didn't get reported on during the week.

I walked in that Monday morning as usual saying, "Good Morning," to my early morning co-workers, those scheduled to be there at 7:00 am. She arrived about 30 minutes after me. I usually gave her about five minutes to set her items down and check her voicemail, before walking into her office.

I got up and knocked on her door. She greeted me with her usual smile, and we exchanged pleasantries. We went through the agenda I prepared and prior to the end of the meeting, I let her know that I needed to share something with her.

I pulled the envelope out of my notebook and handed it to her. She looked at me and asked, "What's this?" I told her that this is my official resignation letter, and that I was putting in notice. Now, me being an author and having a business was no surprise to my manager. I was open with her, and she knew that I was helping people write books. At the same time, I was also part owner of a commercial recording studio.

She was familiar with the businesses that I had. I also had a few co-workers who purchased books from me. It was no secret that I was working other side hustles. And it was never a problem, nor would I let it be because I didn't want anything to disrupt my nine-to-five. I think this is an important lesson.

Sometimes, when we are building our side hustles, we can get a little too lax when it comes to our nine-to-five. We don't handle ourselves properly, or we fall behind on our daily work. While you're working you want to make sure that you're being a good employee and that you are doing the job that you are getting paid to do.

My friend J Haleem says, *"You have to have an entrepreneurial mindset to be a good employee."* This is especially true as I believe many of us are working on our side hustles. All this means is that you have to be willing to devote good and positive energies to both. On both sides of that coin, you need to be able to take care of what you need to take care of. Some of my co-workers were supportive of me and my books. Well, when I walked in, and gave her my resignation, she was shocked, completely taken aback. I am sure she wasn't expecting that and honestly, prior to six months ago, neither was I.

However, I told her that it was time for me to fully devote myself to the business that I was building. I even told her about the spiritual aspect because I knew that she was a believer and would understand it from that space as well. We finished our conversation, talked more about it, and then I went on about my day. I told her that we could let the staff know whenever she was ready to. I thanked her and left her office.

Before I walked out, she let me know that I needed to go and speak with Melanie, the Director of my Department and inform her of my decision. Like my manager, she too was supportive I appreciate the fact that they both wished me well and told me that if I ever needed to come back, I could. I was an employee in excellent standing who always met and/or exceeded expectations in multiple areas. While I appreciated the offer, somehow, I knew I would not ever want to return.

My Director echoed my Manager's sentiments and thought that we would wait a bit before we told the staff. However, later on that day, around 2:00 p.m. in the afternoon, my manager gathered all of the staff together, stating that she had an announcement to make. I walked toward our meeting area, (a small kitchen in the back), with my "poker face," on, but internally I was smiling. I can't remember the exact words she used at this moment, but it went something along the lines of – we have someone leaving that is going on to pursue bigger and better things. She may have even mentioned entrepreneurship, but as I stated, I can't remember.

Everyone was so happy. It was truly a moment for celebration. One of my coworkers asked me about health insurance. She stated that she had thought about starting a side hustle and recognized that the only thing keeping her on the job was health insurance. I said,

"Well, I'm not concerned about that right now," which I now know I should have been. I should have been concerned about more than health insurance to be honest with you. I was so focused and committed to being a book coach full- time that I wasn't concerned about the practical things.

And this is another lesson for those of you reading this book that are going to be starting your business. You have to be concerned about normal, everyday life. You have to have a plan. This is one of the reasons why I'm writing this book and that is to share with you my experiences and help you understand, how important planning is.

Now, I'm not saying that anybody has to get out here and start a business the way that I did, but no matter how you choose to start, you have to have a plan. I told her I wasn't worried about it. I was honest, I was simply ready to step into my next.

The hiring process immediately began. My role was pivotal in the department, and it was important that someone was hired so that I could answer any questions they had and possibly participate in their training. I was able to sit in on a few interviews and talk to individuals about the position and answer any questions that they had. And at the same time training staff who were going to take up some of the responsibilities now that I would no longer serve in that position.

March 31st finally arrived, and I walked in as usual, prepared to my work my last full day. My manager and I planned to go to the warehouse to get some office equipment and to look for other items, such as wall art, and lamps that we could use for decoration. As we were preparing to leave the warehouse, she said, *"You know what, you don't have to work your whole day. How about after lunch, you head on out?"* I asked her if she was sure, and she said that she was.

I told her thank you, but that she didn't have to, I was more than willing to complete the day. She insisted and we were able to have lunch at a Pizza Hut located directly across the street, from the hospital.

After we finished eating, I hugged her, we walked across the street, so that I could say my final goodbyes. I thanked them for all of their love and support shown to me. That was my last day serving as a full-time employee.

CHAPTER SIX

Day One

April 1, 2017, I began my journey into full-time entrepreneurship. It was hard to believe. Now, let me say this. I did not immediately start working. LOL. Yes, I know I had been building my business on the side for a few years. Frankly, this was only a continuation, but I was also leaving a job. I wanted to have that break between ending a job and the side hustle into the new beginning of starting my own business.

As I result, I took the week off. I took that first week off and I slept in. I slept a lot. I got plenty of rest, but that rest also allowed my mind to be free, to strategize, plan, and identify what I wanted the next full week to look like. Unlike most folks, I wasn't projecting three or six months down the road. I wanted to plan the next seven days and make sure that I was setting myself up to be positioned properly.

This was important to me because I believe that how you start is indicative of how you finish. Therefore, if you have a plan going in, you'll take that same mentality, thought processes and energy and you'll carry them throughout the rest of your business. I did a lot of that. I went out and purchased a whiteboard. One that I could hang in the kitchen.

I love whiteboards. If you know me, then you know, I always want to plan and write and draw out and create things on a white board. That's as true for me today as it was back then. As I stated before, I had a full roster of clients. I would get up every day and put their names on the board. I would write out my schedule for the week and what I needed to get done by the end of the week. I had my plan. All of this was good. I rested. Took care of myself. Came off of social media and had some one-on-one time with me to focus.

I needed this time so that when I started that following Monday, I would be ready to hit the ground running. Another thing that I had set to do that first week was some video training. I believe I did a

Facebook live to talk about my journey into' full- time entrepreneurship.

Five years ago, Facebook live was first coming on the scene and I, like many of its other users, had been given creative license to livestream. As a matter of fact, the day that I submitted my resignation to my boss, I did a Facebook live outside on a park bench at the job. The caption of that video was, *"Today, I fired my boss."* During that live, I shared my brief journey.

I shared the experience. I shared the prayer that I prayed. And I shared the fact that when I prayed, God gave me an answer. He gave me the specific date. Back then, saying you "fired your boss," was cool. It was the buzz word and the language that was used whenever anyone took the plunge into entrepreneurship. They would say this along with, "Get rid of your J.O.B. *(just over broke)."*

I engaged in all of that rhetoric and did all of those things. While it was really cool to say, I didn't want to put fluff out on social media. I actually wanted to do something about it and make this full-time entrepreneurship journey really work for me. I was the first person in my family to step into this space. There were no examples laid before me.

In my family, this was a blueprint that I was creating and hopefully making an example for those in my family who may at some point, have this same desire. I will say that getting started, I had my family's support. I had the support of my friends and the community that I had been building since 2015, *Self-Assured Woman*.

Self-Assured Woman was an amazing community filled with women from all over the world and all walks of life. Over the course of the past couple of years, we had held multiple teleconferences, tele-summits, and had virtual presentations from some of the greatest people in my network. Fellow coaches and community leaders, whose missions and values were in alignment with Self-Assured Woman Movement. We covered such topics as building a powerful self-esteem, owning our power as women, walking boldly in our self-assurance, and knowing and understanding what that meant.

I'll never forget the day that this community was birthed in my heart. I was a member of a Facebook community titled, Coach, Speak, and Serve, and on a Sunday afternoon, I was a guest on the Cynthia Hardy Radio Show on the BIG DM 101.3FM station. The Sunday that I was a guest, the topic was domestic violence, and I was brought on to share my survivor story. After the end of my segment, she encouraged me and said, "Tamika, you're a very self-assured woman. I'm happy you're here."

That following Monday, the leader of that Facebook group did a livestream telling us that it was imperative that we build our own communities. Her telling us that and me hearing that I was a self-assured woman from a radio host, caused my Spidey senses to tingle. I knew that I would then go on to create this powerful community of women.

Creating Self-Assured Woman was a blessing. It's not easy building a community, and a business, and doing all of this at once. To use today's vernacular, *"It's not really my thing. Do not recommend."* However, I believe in that season that God graced me for what I was doing. There was never a moment, not one where I was physically tired, or it was taxing.

I was fully engaged, energetic, and was immersed in the act of building a following. I was growing and creating a name for myself in the Women's Empowerment space as well as book publishing. It was always an honor to share my journey, as a guest on radio shows, podcasts, and blogs. Looking back now, I see the uniqueness of the position I was in.

I don't believe that we can always see the good that's going to come out of your business while you're building. You spend a lot of time working on it. I can look back today as I'm in the process of writing and releasing this book that I can see and appreciate the energy and I can see the effort that it takes to keeps something like that growing.

CHAPTER SEVEN

Self-Assured Woman (SAW)

The remainder of 2017 was filled with me fully stepping into the role of being a full-time entrepreneur and not only defining what that would look like for me, but also fully stepping into that role. This meant taking care of myself at the same level that I had been, including continuing to maintain an active roster of clients. It was the only thing I had to do, especially since I no longer had to work for anyone.

For the remainder of that year, that was all that I did. A lot of business building and learning.

Much of this I did on my own. I didn't have a business or marketing and sales coach. There was no one to walk me through that process.

Now that I think about it, I won a two-hour strategy session in a contest. I received some ideas for marketing, sales, and other aspects of my business, which was helpful because as I stated, I had no blueprint to follow.

I wasn't connected to people with that level of influence and access who could share information with me and really walk me through it. And while I had built up a nest egg, I didn't understand then, the importance of making that level of financial investment into myself.

Now, I know that that goes against the grain of the traditional advice. Nowadays, most people will tell you to go out, find a business coach, or a strategist and make that investment before you start your business. Looking back, I know that this is important if your business is only an idea in your mind. I am a believer in that concept, however, that's not the way that I did it.

If I could share yet another lesson in this book for you, then it is to get the help that you need. Don't be afraid to hire the help you need especially when you're first starting out because there's so much that you don't know. To be fair, there weren't a lot of people coaching those interested in building book publishing companies, back then, and maybe this factored into my decision of not hiring a business coach. At this point, I can't be sure.

Although the strategy session was valuable, even from a business perspective, I received great advice, it wasn't from someone who had built a publishing business. And I realize how important that level of knowledge would have helped me move to an even greater level.

One of the key takeaways from that session was the ability to create a spreadsheet of things I needed to get started. And for my particular industry, one of the things I had to do was make some specific tweaks. This was all good.

I continued to focus on building my business, learning as much as I could learn about book publishing. It's crazy for me to think that at this point, I had already been published for six years. That time flew by.

I had been growing & thriving in that space. That's the only way that I can describe it. As the saying goes, *"All good things must come to an end."*

In the case of my business, all of the clients I had in the beginning were finished between that time period. And what I realized is that I had no real plan for attracting other clients to come my way. This was also a struggle, and I suffered a great deal financially because outside of taking the leap – I hadn't thought about sustainability.

This is where I had to learn how to diversity my business. One of the other major goals I started working on was planning my first women's empowerment conference, *Self-Assured Woman Live.*

If you have never built a Facebook community, or if you've never had a desire to build a community, then I encourage you to build one. I encourage you to build your tribe. I encourage you to find the people, your people, that are going to be there to support, believe, and lift you up in the times when it can be tough.

It can most definitely be tough, especially in these digital streets where everybody's somebody. I had planned many virtual women empowerment events, but this would be the first that I would create for women to gather in person.

One of the important things I realized when I built my community is that a lot of women spend a lot of time doing things solo. I believe the reason we do things by ourselves is because women don't necessarily trust other women, especially if they have had adverse experiences or moments where they have not felt supported by other women. Or maybe it was another woman that tore them down under the umbrella of "empowerment, but they weren't. In that space, I realized that I wanted to create something that would be unique for the women in Columbia, South Carolina.

My vision was for women to come and gather in a place where they could finally land their plane, where they could finally no longer worry about flying solo, and truly find their space and community, be amongst like minds. Immediately, once the idea hit my head, I knew I would need an event planner and I would promote from within my community.

If you know me, then you know that I'm not much of a planner at all. I'm a free spirit, so, I tend to fly by the seat of my pants. In addition to the planner, I would also need a conference team and committee. I looked no further than the women who were already members of Self-Assured Woman (S.A.W.). Women who had believed in my vision, some of them had been members since the inception. These women not only knew and understood my heart, but I could trust them to see the vision fulfilled. And trust them to be great representatives of SAW.

We would gather from time-to-time to have our planning conversations. I started thinking of the other types of support that would be needed to pull this off and be successful. That next level of support would come in the form of (SAW) Ambassadors. I created an ambassador program because again, I believe in building women up and truly creating a space for all of us to win. This came from my experience of being a domestic violence survivor. It was women, the women around me, the powerful women, who saw me and didn't want me to continue to remain in the space of being a victim. These women were able to call me out of that mindset with their words.

The creation of the Ambassador program came to me, like many of my other ideas. I sat down and began to outline the program. I detailed their responsibilities to the conference and the community, as well as my responsibilities to them as the community leader. I didn't want them to only serve, but to also be served. As such, I created a private, Facebook community where I could pour into them specifically and give them more direct access to me. Along with the creation of the program, an educational component was added to their experience.

The ambassadors were from all over the country. Women from South Carolina, DC, Georgia, Mississippi, Arkansas, and Louisiana. It was truly a blessing to have these women genuinely believe in the vision of SAW Livc and who were so willing to give of themselves.

The culmination of the program was they had an opportunity to join me in Columbia, SC for the conference. They received education and empowerment. They received multiple chances to learn from me, how I show up in certain spaces, positioning themselves for opportunities, and a host of many other things as I was led to do them.

If you're reading this book and are thinking about planning a live event or conference, I encourage you to do so. At the time that this book is being written, we are almost three years of living through the global Pandemic, and much of our world is getting back to work and being "outside."

In addition to planning the event, I also encourage you to look into adding ambassadors to your conference planning mission. This is all to say that without my conference planning team I would've never been able to pull off SAW Live without their assistance and support. While conference planning was going well, the nest egg that I took my time building was dwindling.

Right around October, I started having financial issues. Like I told you, the clients, weren't coming like that. I had to learn that sometimes that happens. You start off strong and you do well. And you believe that the success you enjoyed as a side hustler will automatically carry over into full-time entrepreneurship, and it does- until it doesn't. All of a sudden, you're like, wait a minute. I didn't plan for this. This isn't going the way that I thought it would go and when you compile money issues on top of that, you really start to see and feel your challenges.

My rent was about $1,000 back then and I started struggling to pay it. I found myself borrowing money from family members so that I could stay afloat. I had a very generous landlord, Clay, who would not penalize me for being late, as long as I wasn't too, too late. He wasn't someone that immediately pursued filing for an eviction. If I had to pay later than the time, he was okay with it. I would still have to pay the late fees, but I didn't have to face eviction. You think paying late and having the money to cover the late fees helps you, but it doesn't because the 1st of the month comes when it comes, and that cycle starts all over again.

October's rent was late. November's rent was late. Finally, in the month of December, my landlord had had enough, and decided to file an eviction. I understood. Not only were the rent payments late, but they were being paid later and later in the month. One day, I arrived home and the eviction notice had been taped to the screen door. Embarrassing.

I parked my car, got out, and grabbed it off of the screen door. I took it inside and placed it on the counter. I walked past it for a little while and finally decided to make the calls. My first call was to Clay, and I let him know that I would be out of the house by the end of the month. My next call was to the Sheriff's Office. If you've never been evicted, then the process is that you contact them and respond to the notice. You are given an additional 11 days and you have to be out by the date or face additional consequences.

Here's the thing. It never dawned on me to go and get a job. I, like I'm sure many of you reading this book, try your hardest to let your business take care of you, your business expenses – and your other financial responsibilities. I didn't even entertain the idea of getting something part-time, which could have helped me get back on my feet until the clients start rolling in again. And it should have. I'm not sure where this ranks in the lesson number in this book, but please don't struggle.

There is nothing sexy about the struggle. I know there are a lot of times that we glorify the struggle, and we psyche ourselves up to believe that this is a great thing. That God is somehow glorified in our struggle. That the struggle means we are doing what we are supposed to be doing.

It means that we're growing the way that we're supposed to be growing. And that is simply not true. I even had to change my mindset about this. You don't have to struggle. My advice is don't put yourself in a position that I put myself in many times because once you lock yourself into this and more importantly this mindset, it becomes extremely hard to get out of. The struggle is almost never locked into one situation.

There have been so many times over my journey of full-time entrepreneurship, where I should have gotten a job, but I didn't. Here's my other piece of advice, "Get a job." If I would have that mindset back then, my life would have changed – but then, maybe you wouldn't have this book in your hands, and I would not have this story to tell. The list goes on of the negatives that could have been avoided.

And don't forget that I'm still *actively* planning a women's conference. Nothing stopped in my life. I lost my house. I was struggling financially. And I had to keep going with this conference. I never even had the thought of cancelling or postponing it. You know why? I've never been a fan of that. I realize now that this is an ego thing. Even though my life was in shambles, not showing up for the women at that event – was not an option.

At this point, I had registrations coming in from across the United States. Women were making plans to fly in, drive in or take a train. Registrations had been purchased from women living in Florida, DC, Maryland, New York, and Little Rock, Arkansas. I was also concerned of people thought. I was making a name for myself, not only in South Carolina, but other parts of the world.

This was my first live event for a thriving women's empowerment community, and I couldn't see it through? It felt as though I would be going against everything I taught, thought, and believed. And I didn't want to fail. Hindsight is always 20/20. What I know now is that I should have never continued on with it.

I was grateful for the sponsorships that were coming in. The seed money that helps offset the costs. It was truly because of them that the conference was able to continue. Outside of continuing on with it, I didn't have a plan. I didn't know what I was going to do. The reality of my life at that time was that the end of 2017 found me evicted out of my home. At the beginning of 2018, with my first live event being held a few weeks later, I found myself living in my commercial recording studio.

CHAPTER EIGHT

Homeless

Self-Assured Woman Live was a phenomenal experience. It was magical. It was beautiful. It was filled with so much love and anyone in that room felt the presence of God in that place. Every time I think about that experience and every time, I think about all of the women who traveled near and far, some even bringing their husbands, I am overwhelmed and in awe of God and how He moves.

I'm extremely grateful for those ladies that thought it not robbery to show up, speak, sit on a panel, host, set up lunch and breakfast and do anything needed in between. And for my ladies who participated in the anthology project *A Woman's Journey to Self-Assurance*, I am grateful to them for allowing me to share and publish their stories. This is my way of continuing to honor them and their sacrifice, love, generosity, and willingness to share and give of themselves.

After the conference was over and after all of the sponsors had been thanked and everybody went back to their respective places in the world, I had to go back to my respective place, which was living in the studio. My work with the commercial recording studio began a little after Ink Pen Diva started. I saw this as an opportunity to enter into the music and entertainment space. Music, in addition to writing, has also been a love of mine. This is something that traces back to my childhood. When I found myself without a home because of the eviction, the studio was the place that I landed. Now, as you are reading this, you may be wondering where my family was and if I had anyone else who could help. My mom lived in Columbia, but her home only had one extra bedroom.

My sister and her sons were living there, which meant that this was not an option for me. As a result, I didn't have any place else to go. The studio had a room in it with a bed, well, it was more like a room that was made to include a bed. The original purpose for the bed was soundproofing the recording booth. It was a tight space and uncomfortable, but I made it work.

Because of this there were certain sacrifices I had to make for my living arrangements. I also still had my business to run, which meant conducting client calls, and if my client lived in Columbia, I took in-person meetings.

At the same time, if there was an artist that we were working with who needed to use the studio, I would have to wait to go to sleep or take care of my other personal needs. Nobody knew that I was actually living there, they only thought I was sitting through the sessions. My personal life was my own cross to bear.

This is another reason that I'm grateful to have an opportunity to write this book because it has done a lot for me in the process of putting it altogether. *Ink Pen Diva* is personal to me. It is me giving more of my myself, and in a strange way, it's also giving me something that I've always needed, but didn't know that I did. That was to release all that I have held bottled up inside.

While dealing with the issue of being homeless, I met a gentleman who I would eventually go on to date. He was a bass player in the band of one of the Gospel artists we were producing. After seeing him in a few sessions, we connected on social media. I believe it was Instagram. He sent a DM and that was how we started talking and conversing before exchanging phone numbers. He worked third shift at a factory about an hour away, which didn't yield itself to much conversation time.

This went on for a couple of months and at his next opportunity of being off from work on a weekend, we had our first date. This date led to a few more. Not soon after he asked me to be his girlfriend. The relationship did not last for many reasons, mostly because his living situation nor mine was conducive to us having a fruitful relationship.

He was there the night I was told that I was going to have to leave the studio. Once I was told to leave – he also left. He left without caring about my wellbeing if he could take me somewhere or anything. He had a home to go to, and I did not. And It was at that point that I decided this relationship was no longer for me.

It was close to Midnight, and to make matters worse, it was the eve of my birthday. It was storming. I grabbed the trash bags I had my clothes in, sat in my car, which was not operable at the time, and called my friend Al. The rain seemed to be in sync with the tears streaming down my face.

Al lived about 15 minutes away and while he was entertaining friends at his home, he dropped everything to come and rescue me. He had a small apartment but allowed me to take the extra bedroom and/or the couch. It was on Al's couch that I sought redemption.

I canceled every appointment I had and laid there for a week. I showered every other day. I was no stranger to the bottom and having to climb my way out of things, but this was different. I hadn't ever experienced such personal losses at the same time, and all within the same year, approximately six months of each other. I didn't know what to do nor with the situation I found myself in, but I knew that that was it. I had given too much of my power over and it was time for me to make a change.

After that week of laying around, I started apartment hunting. This seemed to go on forever. I looked for places for almost 45 days. The very last apartment complex, I looked at – provided acceptance. This was a big deal because I was able to get it as a person who worked for herself! Finally, there was a silver lining.

I would now have a place to call my own. I had only a few things in storage from my previous house, so, I only started off with a bed. I had no living room furniture or kitchen area to eat on. Eventually, my sister brought me a folding table and chairs, and this would become my workspace and eating space. I did this until I could do better. And better was a long way off.

Being in that apartment gave me another start, a fresh start. And I needed that at the moment. I had fallen into a deep depression, a state of despair. And I needed something to help me get back to myself again. The rest of that year, I spent in a broken state. I still struggled financially. The only true blessing that I could see was having breath in my body, and with that, a chance to do it over again each day. I never lost my mind, although I felt that way.

While, there were some bright spots, overall, it was a year. I can't even call it a comeback year because I felt very much as if I was still in it and wondered where the hell the comeback was. Although I was homeless, SAW LIVE started 2018 off with a bang, especially with it being my first live event. However, by the time 2018 would be over, it would be anything but good.

CHAPTER NINE

I Won't Starve

Late 2018, an acquaintance referred me to J Haleem. She told me that he would be a potential book client. I did my due diligence on him and saw that he also had a podcast, In the Studio with J Haleem. I remember setting a goal to help more men write and publish their stories and when she mentioned Jay to me, I thought this was perfect. I was very interested in helping him with the book, but also thought this would be a great opportunity to pitch myself to be on the show.

After looking further into it, I thought, oh wow, this is great. I could tell this was an amazing show that was being produced in my area at the time. I was already into my field of book publishing and coaching, as well as coming off of being involved in the music & entertainment business.

I thought it would be a good fit for me to go on and talk about the work that I'd been involved in. I sent an e-mail to the appropriate address that I found on his website and began corresponding, After a few exchanges, our interview was scheduled January 2019.

Now, I'm fresh off of a challenging year and I'm still dealing with living in an apartment that I damn near was getting evicted out of every other month. Still didn't have a car, but I needed to get to his studio. My only option at the time was borrowing from my sister, so, I did what I needed to do to make sure I had access to a car on the day of the interview.

I made sure I planned my outfit. I would do my makeup and hair because it was an on-camera interview, and the only other thing that needed to happen was I needed a fresh fill-in. My nails were in a horrible condition. Now if you know me or have ever met me, then you know I talk with my hands. There would be absolutely NO WAY I would be on camera without a fresh fill-in. I wasn't worried about a pedicure because I was going to put on heels.

About 45 minutes after I got my nails done, I arrived at the studio. I didn't realize he owned the entire building. It was great to see a young, Black man doing his thing in business as well as giving entrepreneurs like me, an opportunity to sit down with him. Walking into the building, I got a chance to formally meet him, and he introduced me to his wife, Emerald. Always the consummate professional, we exchanged small talk and then we got right to business. From the moment we sat down until the end of our conversation, it was great! One of the best interviews I have ever had.

We talked about everything from music and entertainment to books and the power of words. We discussed why artists didn't want to invest in themselves and he even shared stories with me about his previous experience as an artist manager. Our conversation lasted for approximately one hour. After it was over, I had the chance to hang back in his office and we talked about his desire to write a book.

Meeting Jay was a God thing. It was truly Divine timing. Only I wouldn't realize how true this was until later. We talked further about what working together could look like. I shared my process and next steps, including pricing and we decided we would revisit the opportunity. I thanked him again. We got our "usie," prior to my leaving because after all I did borrow a car and it had to be returned.

I think one week later, I made an appointment with him, and we met again at his office. It was a busy work/travel season and as we discussed the time commitment needed, I think we both knew that while he was excited to get this done, some adjustments needed to be made. However, we continued on with our meeting and discussed some programmatic things on my end and on his end with his busy schedule. Towards the end of the day, we signed the contract, and it took us a minute before we could actually reconnect and have a full book work meeting.

We had our first writing session a few weeks later. He already had the title *I Won't Starve* and knowing that going into the process was a huge help. Prior to our meeting, as was my custom, I sent him some homework assignments that he needed to complete. This was a two-page document that asked him to identify his target reader by completing the Target Reader Questionnaire. There was also the mission, vision, and purpose of the book. When we met, we had an opportunity to review that document and so that we could start working on the actual outline for the book.

The one thing about Jay is that whatever you ask him to do, he will. Any homework assignment he had to complete; it was completed in a timely manner. In addition to the foundational document, he had already completed *I Won't Starve's* dedication, acknowledgements, and introduction. He was definitely ready for the journey that was ahead of us.

After all, this had been his dream for a few years at that point. In fact, prior to our meeting, Jay had started the process, a total of four times. I was then, and still am honored, to finally be the person chosen to help him bring his book to life.

Once the outline for the book was completed, it was on from there. Our meeting of when this was developed, was absolutely amazing. Now that we had the outline, we could finally go forward As mentioned before, it was quite the busy travel season for him. Jay didn't have a whole lot of time for us to have meetings. He was literally being flown across the country for work every week.

One of the things I discovered about Jay is that he had this freaky routine of getting up at 5:00 am and he would go and bring in the sunrise at Starbucks getting more work done in those two hours than anyone else I knew. This meant that in order for me to effectively work with him, I had to get up at 5:00 am. Literally, this is when the text messages and sometimes phone calls would start. Our first chapter meeting day arrived, and we were supposed to meet at Starbucks, however, I didn't have a car, and could not get a ride. We didn't want to miss the opportunity to get this chapter completed, so rather than going to Starbucks, he offered to bring Starbucks to me.

I invited him to my home. This was the first time I had ever invited a client to my place. Jay was not a creep, so I was not worried about anything adverse happening. He brought me a cup of Starbucks as he promised. I never felt uncomfortable in his presence. I was "naked & unashamed," figuratively speaking. He walked in, I had no shoes on, still with my folding table & chairs. I believe the table even had a dip in it, and he sat right down, and we got right into it. We sat and talked for a couple of hours that day.

After this conversation, Jay's interaction with me changed. He *saw* me. And when I say he saw me, I mean, he saw through the challenges I was facing. He saw my potential. He saw my knowledge. He saw gifts, that I didn't know I possessed – underneath it all. It was at that point, he said that we could forgo the book project, and I could help him in another area, which was managing him. I couldn't see it. I appreciated the vote of confidence, but the problems before me were way to grand.

As a result, we chose to move forward strictly with working on the book. As I mentioned earlier, Jay had tried this four times before. Everyone he had prior, he wanted them to write the book for him. Even when it came to his schedule, I was like there's no way you're that busy. To prove his point, he gave me a brief look at his calendar, and I had to eat my words. He was in fact, as busy as he said he was. I still wasn't convinced, there was no way I was going to ghostwrite a project.

The reason is because the premise of Ink Pen Diva's writing coaching program was to coach and support authors to birthing their own book baby. It was never created in the space of me ghostwriting. I had no desire to be a ghostwriter. My passion for that came from my wanting the authors that chose to work with me, to empower them to use their own voices. Nothing is more powerful than the pen, and along those same lines, nothing is more powerful than our voices.

This was the reason for our back & forth. I was encouraging him to write the book so that it could be in his own voice. This way, he could tell the story the way he wanted it to be told in a manner that only he could. I would teach and guide along the way, edit for grammar and context, and make sure he would produce a work he would be proud of.

We went back and forth for weeks. And while we were able to make some progress, it wasn't as much as it could have been. Flexibility was such a struggle for me back then. The program was the program. The process was the process. If you didn't follow it, then I was not the coach for you. However, as not to delay the book writing any further, I agreed. He had been telling me all along, but I was too busy trying to stick to the script.

And I needed to be flexible with him in order to have a level of understanding and be aware of what was going on with him as well as myself. Finally, I agreed to serve as his ghostwriter. As you can determine, *I Won't Starve* was the first and last project that I ever or will ever serve as the ghostwriter for. Writing *I Won't*

Starve was amazing. There was so much that I learned about me, and he learned about him.

The one area that I experienced tremendous growth in was writing. I consider myself a writer, I always have. I love the written word. I'm also a reader. Most good writers love to read. *The Plus Factor*, my first book was published in 2011. And at the time that I met him, it had been seven, almost eight years since that book was released, which means that was the last time I wrote a story of that magnitude.

How I wrote *The Plus Factor* was completely different than how we were writing *I Won't Starve*. When I wrote *The Plus Factor*, I was focused only on telling the story and giving a voice to victims of domestic violence in the faith community. I got it out and I enjoyed great early success with it. When it came to ghostwriting his story, I had never experienced that particular writing style before.

I Won't Starve was off to a great start. While we were working on the book, Jay noticed that I was running my business off of a cellphone and broken computer. I thought nothing of this. I didn't think it was anything special. This was an example of me figuring it out. I was completely surprised when he told me that this was one of the things he admired about me. My ability to still do what I needed to do, in spite of what he saw me going through.

Even though he admired that, he thought it was urgent that I fixed some of those problems. One of those was me needing new headshots. I hadn't had pictures of me taken since 2014. So much about me had changed and these were extremely outdated. Because he saw what I was going through, he gave me a headshot session for free! Talk about a gift.

Jay's customer service is top notch. When I received my pictures 24 hours later, my mind was blown. I had never gotten anything back that fast. Me being the social media person I am, I immediately shared this picture on my timeline. People went crazy! I had almost 1,000 likes and lots of shares. My picture was even shared as an example of what to do with professional photography. I was blown away. The only time I've ever received that many likes was on a "Happy Birthday," post.

In addition to this great blessing, I was about to walk into another one. March 2019, one of my Self-Assured Woman Movement community members and former Ambassadors asked me to not only speak at her first live event, but to serve as the keynote. I had only done one other keynote speaking engagement several years prior.

Imagine my joy when my former Ambassador asked me to keynote her first live event. Her event was held in Spartanburg, SC, which was about an hour and a half away from Columbia. My sister and I made the day trip on a Saturday, (remember, I still don't have a car), so she had to take me. I walked into that building and was immediately greeted. I was treated like royalty because they were expecting my presence and they prepared a place for me. She did an amazing job putting on that event, which was also her first conference. This was definitely a full circle moment.

Right about this time, I started making plans to conduct a Book Writing & Publishing Workshop titled, *Get Write & Get Published*. It was going to be held at Converspace, which at the time was a co-working space in Columbia, SC. I got a nice flyer designed, created a landing page, and began marketing the event.

What I didn't realize is that something sinister was in the mix. Out of nowhere, I started being tagged in vile and threatening posts on social media. An account had been created with no other posts, but recent pictures of me. Whoever created this account started messaging friends of mine, and asking how well they knew me, and that they were going to share information about me.

I initially thought to ignore it. This went on for weeks. At one point, my safety was threatened, and I contacted the Richland County Sheriff's Department, Cyber Crimes Division. A very nice female deputy showed up to my apartment. I had screenshots and kept messages that had been sent to me. Because no physical harm had occurred, there wasn't much that the sheriff's department could do.

She told me to continue to keep a record of anything that happened, and if it escalated to give them a call again. I felt so alone. I didn't deserve what was happening. For the most part, I was a quiet person who stuck to themselves, and never bothered anyone. I couldn't understand where this was coming from and who in the hell it was. I was angry. I walked in fear because I had no idea where this person could be. I felt alone, but I wasn't. Jay was there.

I called him on a Saturday evening and told him that I was afraid, and I didn't know what to do. He immediately made his way to me. Him and the family. He pulled up on me to make sure that I was okay. Jay and I were truly building our bond, and this was one of many examples of him proving his friendship to me.

We were getting closer to the day of the workshop, and I was still getting threatening messages. I knew then that I was going to have the workshop, but I would hire private security. I reached out to a gentleman I knew. I explained to him what had been happening and that I would need his services the day of the event that would be held in May. He was an armed security officer, so I knew if anything popped off or if the person threatening me showed up, I would be physically protected.

Get Write & Get Published, went off without a hitch. I even had people show up the day of and purchase a ticket. It was amazing. I hadn't had a book writing workshop since 2017. I even signed on some clients that day. Whoever was threatening me, never made an appearance. I reported the account and any others that may have surfaced and as soon as it began, it was over. Make no mistake that this was a very scary experience. I went home that day exhausted, but full. There is something about being in front and amongst the people that I absolutely love.

As we continued the work of I Won't Starve, I realized that it was equally as challenging to Jay as well. At one point, he even wanted to quit. In fact, he said the words, *"I don't want to do this shit anymore."* My response was, *"I'll call you later."* I wasn't going to let him quit, so we persevered. This was life-changing, and we had to fight through whatever we had to fight through to get this book to the finish line.

Soon after, we agreed to co-write the book, we became even more focused and drilled down on a more specific plan to help us bring *I Won't Starve* to life. With the focus, came the need for adjustments and changes. One major adjustment I was still struggling with was the time I had to get up in the morning.

I told you guys that Jay is an early riser. He was up at 5:00 am every morning, which meant I needed to be up and ready to go at 4:45 am every morning. I made sure to charge my computer the night before and have it open and ready to go along with pen and paper to jot down any notes I needed. Oh, and coffee, can't forget coffee.

Midway through the year, the lease at my apartment was ending, and it was time for me to find another place to live. At this point, Jay and I had become fast friends. I still didn't have a car to get around, so true to his nature - he was kind enough to come and pick me up on multiple days and take me around to do some apartment hunting.

Prior to going out and looking for new apartments, I made a vow to myself. I affirmed prior to leaving, that once I moved, I would NEVER go another month paying the rent late and that I would always have food. I didn't know how I was going to do this, but what I did know is that I would no longer live how I had been living.

Where the first time for apartment hunting took me about 45 days, this next time around, it would only take me two weeks. I was locked and loaded and able to move-in, July 1st. Once inside of that apartment, I got reorganized in my life and business. I pulled out the white board. I looked at my financials. I looked at my client base. I knew how many clients I would need to bring on and the services I needed to market to make this happen. I had to go hard.

The work on *I Won't Starve* never stopped. One day in September, he, Emerald, and I went out to lunch. During that time, she began talking with me about some of the growth and changes in Jay's businesses. After she finished sharing, I was formally asked to join the team in a more permanent manner.

One of the first events I had a chance to participate in was the *I Won't Starve Entrepreneur Development Workshop.* It was going to be held the first Saturday in October. I had been hearing about the experience since the beginning of the year. The workshop was held twice a year, once in the Spring and once in the Fall.

This particular workshop was special because we chose this day as the beginning of pre-order sales for Jay's new book. The day arrived and I got a chance to see the magic at work. We had staff, vendors, and volunteers. Emerald made sure everything was coordinated properly. No detail was overlooked. The workshop was held at Midlands Technical College in their theatre, and it was standing room only.

Once we announced that folks could pre-order that day, we had a line of people wrapped around the entrance. I had never seen this before! He had truly built up a name for himself and had an amazing following of I Won't Starve. This was what support looked like. This really blew my mind. I knew he had something special, and I was glad to be a part of it!

After the workshop was over, we spent the next couple of weeks doing readings and making the necessary edits. It was important to Jay that we did not write a tabloid or tell anyone else's story but his. Once the overall process was complete, we were able to produce the book that has changed the lives of thousands. There is no way I can write this portion of my story without sending big love and giving J Haleem his flowers for the opportunity he gave me.

If you know anything about ghostwriting, then you know that most of them don't get credit, by having their names mentioned in the books they write. I was of the same mindset that I would follow the rules. It was not industry standard.

However, true to his nature, he encouraged me to put my name in it. He was adamant about it because ultimately it took nothing away from him or his story. I am grateful he helped stretch me in an area that I had never been stretched in. I count it as a blessing.

Because of the amazing work we did with *I Won't Starve*, and the level of personal growth I experienced, 2019 was incredible. Not only did I meet him and make a new friend, but I was also able to connect with his wife, meet his family, and as a result, I extended mine.

I Won't Starve was published November 15, 2019. About one week later, I received an e-mail from the City of Columbia's Office of Business Opportunities. The e-mail stated that I had been recommended to recccivc an application to participate in the upcoming cohort of FASTTRAC® sponsored by the Kauffman Foundation.

FASTTRAC® is a 10-week program for entrepreneurs. Participants learn everything from marketing and sales to money management and brand building. Because of Jay's relationship with the City of Columbia, I was able to receive a scholarship for this program. I submitted the application to participate and waited to hear back.

Now it was time to prepare for the book release event. We had secured a venue downtown Columbia, a nice and neutral location. This was to be the celebration of all celebrations and it was! We had the entire upstairs of this restaurant that was already equipped with a stage, food, and space for a DJ. Jay gave me the honor of doing a reading from *I Won't Starve* and share for the first time publicly a portion of the book's content. Jay was even interviewed on the stage by his best friend.

In my opinion, this is how a book release should be done. Once the program was complete, it was time to dance and time for him to sign books. His first experience as an author. Most of my clients had written a book before building a brand, that wasn't the case with him. Jay had spent years building I Won't Starve, as a brand, a book was the only missing piece.

CHAPTER 10

Executive Assistant

Once the celebration was over, it was time for me to get to work. Getting prepared for this book release, our calendar went crazy. Ink Pen Diva as a business was suffering because of my work with J Haleem.

Earlier in the year, I had an opportunity to travel to Asbury Park, NJ. My then client, Pastor Stephanie Lashley and I scheduled a book-writing workshop to help some of her congregation and local community who were interested in writing a book. Once this one was over, she and I started talking about another. It was planned for later in the year, I knew this time Jay would accompany me. I would have him speak on book marketing and sales. This would be a great addition to my workshop and a great way for me to get him some exposure.

My relationship with Pastor Stephanie made it easier to coordinate a signing as well as speaking opportunity for him. However, I knew that we would also have to "beat the street," and introduce him to new audiences in new communities. That speaking opportunity was in New Jersey. I knew we needed to get him in front of more people in South Carolina. First up was Charleston.

I had had an opportunity to travel to Charleston with Jay. He was asked to speak at an event sponsored by the City of Charleston, alongside of Mayor Tecklenburg. Once that event was over, we stopped by several bookstores and inquired about in-person signings. His pull-up game is definitely strong!

We decided to go old school and go door-to-door. We hit several bookstores, one of which was *Blue Bicycle Books*. I walked in and introduced myself and Jay and asked the process for local authors. I hit it off with the salesperson and as it turns out, the store manager was standing right there, quietly working. He responded that they'd love to have him, and he told us what we needed to do. We would even be allowed to leave a couple of copies behind for consignment. This was a huge win and the first time I had ever done anything like this.

From Charleston, I started looking for independent bookstores throughout the state of South Carolina. We were going to get this book out to the masses by any means necessary. I found another bookstore in Orangeburg. It was owned by a husband and wife. I did my spiel over e-mail and after a few days of corresponding, another book-signing was scheduled for Jay, in a different city. We were on a roll.

Get Write and Get Published was also on the books for December

2019. Now, of course we couldn't travel all the way to New Jersey for just one event. I did what I do and that is find a local bookstore in Newark, his hometown. Newark is not too far from Asbury Park, so that worked out perfectly. We were able to get him a book-signing downtown Newark, which was amazing. As it turns out the bookstore owner was the aunt of one of his high school friends, what a coincidence. This signing was special because his family and friends who grew up with him could attend an event in their area.

We had also arranged contact with his former high school basketball coach, who coordinated an opportunity for Jay to speak at the school. Of course, we gifted him with a copy of Jay's book. He kept saying how proud he was of him and of this great accomplishment.

The next day arrived, and it was time for Get Write and Get Published – New Jersey. From my past experience with Pastor Stephanic, Jay and I would be speaking in the same place - her boxing gym. I think he was truly surprised at the "stage." I thought it best to split our workshop up into two parts. I would begin with book writing, which is always first in an author's journey. After we took a brief break, Jay would come and do his portion. This proved to be an extremely effective addition to my workshop and increased the value. I had facilitated writing workshops before, but I had never been able to speak to book marketing and sales. He was able to sell books to everyone in that room and I was able to leave with several new clients.

That weekend in New Jersey was a whirlwind, good vibes, great people, and giving us an opportunity to continue to touch and connect. At this point, I had rebranded myself to Get Write With Tamika, but he helped me to understand, see, and get to know who the Ink Pen Diva truly was outside of the moniker. He helped me to understand how important my work was and how much that set me apart from everyone else doing what I did. There were so many highlights of 2019. I was truly existing in the space as Jay's Executive Assistant, and we were making some great strides.

January 1, 2020, I received an e-mail from Tom Ledbetter

welcoming me to the 16th cohort of the City of Columbia's FASTTRAC® Entrepreneur Development Program. Classes began January 16th and would run through the middle of March. Being accepted into this program was awesome and truly a great way to start off the year, but what happened next would be a true moment for life.

Jay received an opportunity to shoot Super Bowl LIV. This Super Bowl would be between the San Francisco 49ers and the Kansas City Chiefs. I was extremely happy for him. Jay was a commercial photographer, and this was a big deal to be able to work directly with the NFL.

To my surprise, he asked me to make the trip with him. I could not believe it! The game was going to be held in Miami. I had never been to any NFL game before, but a chance to go to the Super Bowl? WOW!

It would not only be my first opportunity to go to Miami, but this would also mean that I would have to be screened, in order to get press credentials. This was a cool process for me to experience and get a behind-the-scenes look. I provided all of the information needed to Emerald as she was coordinating the details.

I could barely contain my excitement about this trip. It was crazy that so many good things were happening all at once. It's the week of Miami trip and we were swamped. The weekend prior was the book-signing at *Blue Bicycle*

*Books. Blue Bicycle Book*s was ready for us. As soon as we walked into the door, they had a flyer with Jay's picture on it on the door, and a small table with more signs and a copy of his book. The goal I set was accomplished, I wanted to introduce him to new people, and we did.

While it was a successful event, it was also somber. We found out walking into the bookstore, that Kobe Bryant and his daughter Gianna died in a plane crash. I believe that not only would we all remember this, but so would the rest of the world.

That following Tuesday it was time for Jay to speak in Charlotte, NC at the high school I had arranged for him. This was truly a great experience as he was off to a great start building his platform as an author. We had to hurry up and get back to Columbia, that day because later on that evening, was my first FastTrac® class. The very next morning we were leaving for Miami. I had heard so much about it from Jay, mostly about the beautiful weather. I learned that Miami was a city he and Emerald enjoyed going to.

When we arrived, it was beautiful and sunny in the mid-80s in January. We had approximately two hours from the time we received our press passes, until it was time to meet the players at our first event. I remember Jay and I running through the check-in center. Once we arrived, we had to find the press area, get checked in, show our IDs, and receive our press passes. We ran through that place. After receiving our press passes, we found someone to take our picture in front of the Super Bowl sign and ran again back to the car.

First up were the San Francisco 49ers. When we walked into the room, we observed that all of the major national & international media & news outlets were there. Broadcast networks such as ESPN, Fox Sports, CBS Sports, NFL Network, and then there was also, J Haleem Media.

While I know that I was supposed to be getting "B roll footage," I couldn't help but enjoy the eye candy that was in the room in front of me. I got an up close and personal look at some of the most handsome men you could ever see. They were tall and truly blessed by God in the body department. I found myself looking and staring when I was supposed to be working. Jay caught me and gave me this look like, "Hello! We are supposed to be working here." I mouthed sorry and got back focused.

I watched him do what he does best as a media personality and that is go around the room getting interviews, asking questions to the players that were being interviewed live, and doing sit-downs with some of his favorites. Most notably included Deebo Samuel, and Jimmy Garoppolo. Richard Sherman was playing for the 49ers at the time and since they are fraternity brothers, Jay was able to get a picture with him. This picture still hangs on his office wall. Our time with the

49ers lasted approximately two hours. After that, we were free to go about the city and explore a bit, but first – food!

All the way to Miami, Jay talked about this particular restaurant that he loved, *Finger Lickin'*. We had been working all day and we were hungry. *The Lickin'*, as it was now called was a great restaurant that served a combination of seafood and soul food. You could get collard greens and macaroni and cheese, or seafood rice.

It was everything he talked about and baby this food was delicious. I had macaroni and cheese, candied yams, and fried chicken. When we sat down to eat, we didn't say one word to each other. Our lips were smacking.

I got up early the next morning and was dressed and out of my room by 7:30 am. Jay was already waiting downstairs in the lobby. Today, we were to go and get our coverage of the Kansas City Chiefs. He reminded me that I was there to work and not look at the players. I laughed.

Their event was held in a different part of the city, at another luxurious hotel and event center. When I say Miami is beautiful, it is beautiful. All I saw were streets lined with palm trees, and clear, blue skies. After we made it through security check, we walked through the area where the press was gathering and found our place.

We got our coverage with the Chiefs, and we were actually able to get closer to some of the players more so than we were with the 49ers. After we got all of the footage and the coverage that we needed, we grabbed some lunch, once again stopping by The Lickin' of course. This was an *amazing* experience.

Not only did I watch Jay handle his business, but I saw his smile larger than I had ever seen it before. Every ESPN personality that he grew up watching on television, he was not only able to meet in person and get pictures with. He was so happy. It wasn't about work in those moments, it was about him. I hadn't known him that long, but I could tell how much this moment meant to him. And for that matter, how much it would mean to me.

After Miami, we began hearing about this disease, this virus that was impacting other parts of the world that had now made its way to the United States. It was known as the Coronavirus. I didn't think much of it initially. I had worked for a major hospital system during the Bird Flu, Swine Flu, and the Ebola Virus. I remember the great precautions we had to take, coming up with protocols, and hearing about PPE for the first time.

COVID-19 became unlike anything else we'd ever experienced. It was a global Pandemic. There hadn't been a Pandemic since the flu. I never thought that I would ever live through a Pandemic. I remember seeing the images of our medical personnel and those on the front lines. Images of grief, exhaustion, and despair.

At J Haleem, LLC, we had been in the process of planning, *The Perfect Partnership*. A symposium focused on creating strategic partnerships, but there were also workshops and panel discussions on government contracting and protecting your intellectual property to name a few.

Slowly, we started to see events being canceled throughout the city. Our sponsors began inquiring as to whether or not we were going to continue on with our event. Jay called a meeting with us and asked our opinion on what we believe we should do. I mentioned earlier that I am not a fan of canceling events, so rather than taking in the seriousness of what was happening around us, I stuck to my stance, and said we should keep going. Because of my dismissal and lack of focus, I almost damaged a sponsor relationship. I had spoken out of turn and not under advisement from him. Thankfully, Jay was able to quickly rectify the situation.

Little by little, the city began to cancel events. The Perfect Partnership was also canceled. It seems as though right after that; the United States government implemented a nationwide shutdown.

At the time that the shutdown was implemented, I was in my apartment, on the other side of town, with no car. I had a place to stay. I had food. And if I needed to get to a store, a gas station, or a restaurant, pretty much everything was within walking distance. There was a Waffle House on the corner and if I wanted something else, a Burger King was in the opposite direction. I could walk and get to what I needed.

However, with the shutdown, my being able to even walk and get what I needed, became a concern because yes, while I could figure it out, the question became of what resources would be available when I got there. My huge mishap with that company and another private matter caused separation in my professional and personal relationship with Jay. At this point, it was estranged. Yet, he still found it in his heart, to make sure that I was okay and one day he came to see about me.

I was so surprised. He mentioned that he and Emerald had talked and wondered what my plans were? I told him that my plan was to walk to get whatever food I needed. They said the shutdown would only last for a couple of weeks and I didn't want to put anyone out to help me, especially since this wasn't a singular situation. We were all going through this.

Although things were not the best between us, he told me that if I wanted to, I could come stay with them for the next couple of weeks. I accepted the offer, threw whatever I could grab in a bag, and left with him.

181

CHAPTER 11

The Shutdown

Jay and Emerald created a space for me in their home. Two weeks became another two weeks. Now, we are a month in, and I started wondering when this was truly going to end. This would prove to be an adjustment for all of us. At times it was uncomfortable, but together, we made it work. In the season of COVID-19, it seemed as if everyone was doing whatever they had to do.

I don't remember the city being that scarce since the time of the

1,000-year historic flood. The local grocery store became an essential business and its staff, essential workers. This no longer became a term that would apply only to healthcare . The stores never closed, they adjusted their daily schedule. The first hour of their opening was set aside for the elderly to shop. The general public would be allowed in at the beginning of the next hour. This was a smart move on their part because we know the immune systems of the elderly and children could be compromised or not fully developed. Even with the general public coming in, only a certain number of people were allowed in the store at once. When we were allowed entry, we had to have our temperature checked, and had to make sure we were wearing our gloves and face mask.

The next big change for everyone was social distancing. Every one had to stand six feet apart. You couldn't walk down any aisle as you normally would. One aisle was labeled with the up arrow and the other with the down. One entrance was for entry and the other for exiting. This was really an adjustment to everyone's lifestyle and if you weren't paying attention, you would find yourself being turned around or receive the death stare from those who actually were following the rules. With the rules always comes rule breakers.

No matter how much we heard that masks saved lives because COVID was an Airborne illness, there were those who didn't want to wear them. They didn't believe they were being protected from anything. Where there was once a large quantity of masks and gloves, eventually these became hard to find or they had to be ordered. As if gloves and masks weren't enough, the BIG challenge would be finding cleaning supplies and toilet paper.

Immediately, it seemed that once the world was aware that a virus was spreading, cleaning supplies disappeared overnight. You couldn't find Clorox. Pine Sol. Fabuloso. You couldn't even find the generic store brands. Forget about Lysol. Lysol became the hottest commodity.

People were driving all over town to find it and I was one of them. There was a Dollar General in the neighborhood where Jay &

Emerald lived, and we discovered that their trucks came Wednesday night. Knowing this, eliminated a lot of the hassle of driving around town. They would get in approximately 20 cans of Lysol, and it would be available on Thursday morning. However, you had to be in line in order to get it. Every Thursday morning, we were up at 6:45 am to be in line by 7:00 in order to be one of the ones to get the Lysol. We were lucky every week.

Finally, a Facebook friend who worked at Sam's Club posted a picture. They had pallets of Lysol! I hit him in the DM and asked if there was more available and how I could get it? He said as long as you were a member, you could get a case of four! BET! They were members so that made it easy. And this became the Lysol plug! I no longer had to chase Lysol. I only needed to go every week to Sam's and join the never-ending row of folding chairs. Jay, Emerald, and the kids had even developed a "Lysol dance." Whenever I walked back through the doors, they would perform it. Fun times.

Since most conferences were shut down and there weren't many opportunities for training, even virtually, Jay decided to move up the release of his second book, *U Won't Starve: Key Principles for Entrepreneur Development*. Suffice it to say, he had been seriously bitten by the book bug. Writing *I Won't Starve* was always in his plan, *U Won't Starve*, while not previously thought about, made perfect sense to be added to his brand. This was especially true considering the time we were living in. History has shown that many of the businesses we support and are familiar with today, were started during the last Pandemic. This time was no different.

Our writing process for *U Won't Starve:* was completely different than *I Won't Starve.* While we co-wrote *I Won't Starve*, this time around, he took a full stab at writing the book himself and let me tell you he did an amazing job. Having one under his belt made the overall process easier, but we still had to make sure that we presented his principles in a manner that would be easy-to-read for his now growing and thriving audience, insert the Ink Pen Diva. Now, I had finally gotten him to buy into my process.

It was important to him that we not only provided practical tips for entrepreneur development, but also specific examples for the three generations of the workforce that this book speaks to, Gen-Z, Millennials, and Baby Boomers. Even the way he approached the writing of this book was different. Where *I Won't Starve* took us several months to complete, he wrote *U Won't Starve* in 30 days! Talk about lessening the learning curve. While many jobs were shutting down and with the addition of government stimulus money, many new entrepreneurs were born and who better to learn from, than someone that has been in business for more than 20 years? Initially, the release date would be the one-year anniversary of *I Won't Starve*, but it was moved up, so that it would be released on his birthday.

Selling this book would prove to be different. Because of the shutdown, I wasn't able to physically go into bookstores and introduce the books to them. I came up with some new and different ideas. I told Jay that he needed an additional way for people to opt-in to him, so that they could still have access and we could sell this book. He agreed and the *I Won't Starve Nation*, private Facebook community was born.

One of the principles in *U Won't Starve* is Market Research. Because we were living in the Pandemic, many businesses needed to revitalize their tactics. I encouraged him to facilitate a virtual training on this topic. The

Market Research workshop was well attended and on that day he was able to present some much-needed information. This would also be the day that he would open up pre-orders for *U Won't Starve*.

The orders were pouring in. People were truly excited about this book. In this time of uncertainty, many businesses either had to close or pivot. I eventually grew to hate this word. Using some of the tactics that were placed in *U Won't Starve*, we were able to turn up the heat on marketing and promotions. At this point, we were also nearing the end of the school year. Jay decided that everyone needed a break and planned a trip to Tennessee. I had even been invited to go on the trip with them.

This would be my first time going anywhere with the entire family. I was very excited and looked forward to hanging out and getting to know more about them and have some fun. We stayed in a beautiful AirBnB. It was nice to get away and breathe, to get out into nature, pause and reflect, and enjoy us. The week prior, the George Floyd murder happened. While we were in Tennessee, we watched continual news coverage of this and the nationwide outrage. Marches were happening all over the country, even back home in Columbia, SC. On the day of Jay's birthday, we officially released *U Won't Starve*. Throughout the course of the day, we watched as sale after sale came in, eventually leading him to becoming an Amazon #1 Bestselling Author.

I could not contain my excitement. I had never been in the room when any of my clients discovered their status as an Amazon bestselling author. We were truly celebrating in that place. And to be in the room, as his entire family surrounded him with love was everything. This was an amazing accomplishment even for me and put me on another level as a book writing coach. I was definitely getting to the bag. In the words of Fat Joe, "Yesterday's price was not today's price."

Throughout the shutdown, I had been going back and forth to my apartment to check on it and make sure everything was good. Now that things were lifted, I was able to go back home. On our workdays, I would meet Jay at his office.

One of the other great projects we began working on that year, was Volume 1 of the *Anti-Bullying Series*. This was special to me because the author, Sydney Jo, Jay's daughter Sydney had launched the Anti-Bullying Club, her 501c)3 nonprofit organization some years prior, and with the Pandemic she was unable to have the meetings for which she had grown accustomed.

Drawing on the inspiration from her father, Sydney decided that she wanted to publish her first book, *Malaysia's BIG Move*. And she asked me to help her write the book. I was excited and ecstatic. I've worked with children before, but never this close. Working with Sydney was a lot of fun. It was very *teenagerish*. Is that even a word?

Sydney made this process all her own. I would even venture to say that she threw herself into it. We pulled out the whiteboard once again and was able to complete her outline that way. Once approved by Jay and Emerald, we began the writing process.

She would be laid out on the conference room table, doing flips down the hallway, and dancing. I didn't stop her. Jay would look at her sometimes and shake his head. We were able to get this book done in no time, with plenty of cartwheels and flips to prove it. I was getting used to a more hands-on approach. I found myself doing more contributing rather than critiquing.

U Won't Starve was still going strong. Going after speaking engagements were different now. Although most of the world was virtual, this presented even more opportunities for me to get speaking engagements for him in bigger markets. I came across a national organization titled Main Street America. I discovered that they had a local chapter in Kershaw, South Carolina. Once I did some deeper digging into their mission and work, I saw a synergy with J Haleem, LLC.

I reached out to her, introducing myself and told her about Jay and the work that he was doing in the community. She invited us to submit a proposal outlining exactly what we could provide along with pricing. This let me know that I could do this everywhere. This helped me to not only finetune my pitch but expand the markets I was reaching out to. I found that there were no geographical boundaries with virtual opportunities.

Once he did this, I knew I could talk to people all over. I was able to book jobs for him primarily on the West Coast. This worked out great because as I was booking jobs Jay and the family were planning to take a trip to California late that Summer. I was even able to line up some meetings for him while they were out there. I was still handling business in South Carolina, but also took this opportunity to spend time with my family.

When they got back, I was full speed ahead on planning the book release for Sydney Jo. I created a press release that lead to her being interviewed on local news stations as we were building the buzz and getting the word out in the community. Even though we were still in the Pandemic, Sydney was able to have her book signing at Jay's office. Everyone wore masks and we did temperature checks, but at least she was able to have the full experience that she watched her dad have one year prior. *Malaysia's BIG Move* was officially released in October, which is recognized nationally as Bullying Prevention Month.

The release of Sydney Jo's project reignited the spark in my business. I'm going to be honest here – I had lost all momentum. I didn't think I could continue to work my business and also serve as Jay's Executive Assistant. Because he had a larger brand and was much further along in business than me,

I chose to focus solely on helping him.

I remember him having a tough conversation with me one evening. One in which he encouraged me to continue to be who I am and do the work that I was doing when he met me. Frankly, Jay never asked me to stop my business. In fact, because I now had two very gifted individuals around me, that should have been my sign to keep going and keep climbing higher, instead I took it as a reason to do the exact opposite. That conversation was what I needed, and I gained another level of respect for him.

This led to the creation of *Start 2021 Off Write!* I needed to get back to me and doing what I love. Not only is that helping authors to write their books, but it was also educating aspiring authors on that process and what it entails. At this point it was a little more than two years since my last workshop in 2019, and it was time for me to put myself back out there as the expert that I am. It was a four-hour workshop held on a Saturday, while I had a good number of registrants, I wasn't sure how many would hang with me after sitting for so long, but no one left, and the cameras were on! A huge win! I have often said that I should have been a teacher, I really enjoy it.

I realized that no matter what was happening to the world around us, we were alive to experience it, feel it, and be a part of it, even in the midst of being socially distanced and shut down. As my epigraph states, *"There will come a time when you believe, something is ending, and that is the beginning."* I've had beginnings, plenty of them, and endings that have changed my life, but none would compare to what was waiting on me in 2021.

CHAPTER 12

The Decision

Towards the end of 2020, after that conversation with Jay, I started receiving an influx of clients. Now the days leading into December and January, are typically slow months for me. Many families are saving for holiday shopping and/or trips while the kids are out of school for the holidays. Writing a book for all intents and purposes is a passion project. What I know for sure is that investments aren't always made into passion projects. However, business was looking up, I had even ethically raised my prices.

Coming into the beginning of the year, everything was going well. The world had opened back up at this point and things were getting somewhat back to normal. At that time, I had enjoyed great success from the most bestselling book of my career, *U Won't Starve: Key Principles of Entrepreneur Development*. We were still doing our business as usual, and I continued to spend a lot of time at their house. This was also the year that Jay was turning 40 and we were planning a special trip to Jamaica to celebrate it. It would be even more special to me because I would be getting my Passport for the first time.

Everything was going along as planned. One particular weekend in April I was with them and that Saturday morning, Jay came back in from an appointment. He walked in the door and greeted everyone. After he got himself together, he sat down with us and said he had something important that he wanted to discuss. He had our attention for sure. His next words were, *"We are moving to Las Vegas."* I think we all sat there for a minute before responding, and finally, we said, *"OK!"*

We took the rest of the day to talk about this and ask why Vegas? Coming off of the success of *U Won't Starve*, as previously Jay started receiving a lot of love from the West Coast. This included landing a contract with a company out of San Diego. They were already in talks with him to serve as a consultant on the East Coast, but instead he was hired to be a consultant in Southern California. We knew that we would be making a move of some sort and I believe that Emerald and I both kind of thought it would be California. California made sense. Imagine our surprise when he mentioned that the West Coast move would be to Las Vegas.

The following morning, he had went for a walk and when he came back, he actually had the plan of how we were going to get ourselves established out there. We were very intrigued by the idea. When he came back, I realized that a part of that plan was me. Understanding that my business would probably take a bit of a hit going to a new place, he had the forethought to make sure that I would do something that would carry me while we all got acclimated to a new city. Jay had been doing research on careers in Las Vegas. His research showed him that one of the best industries to work in is bartending. He asked, *"What do you think about becoming a bartender?"* *"A bartender?"* I repeated. *"Why would I be a bartender?"*

He carefully explained his thoughts. That while I would be taken care of, he understood that I might not be able to enjoy the amenities I was used to. Bartending would supplement my income and also not take up a lot of time while I was building my community in Vegas. This meant that he would have to build up his community as well, which was understood by all of us.

At this point, Jay had already begun writing his third book titled, *Morning Motivation Consistent Encouragement Through a Crisis.* This was an idea I had given him based on a video series he created under the same name. He had completed more than 150 videos and decided to give it a break. I mentioned the idea to him of how I thought he could expound on the content, and he loved it. Immediately jumping into the process.

Getting back to bartending, your girl loves a cocktail and really enjoys a good red and white wine, but I never thought about or had the desire to actually learn the process and the science behind creating drinks, mixing them, and coming up with cocktail ideas and recipes. However, I am always eager and excited to learn. Once he explained to me why he thought this would be a great position, it was perfect. Being a bartender fits my personality on many levels.

I then asked if there was a class he knew about that I could attend to learn more about it. He happened to have a connection and as it turns out, she was hosting a class that following Saturday through her mixology company. He shared with me her contact information, and I reached out to her, introducing myself and letting her know that I was interested in attending her bartending class. She informed me that she did have space in the class and gave me the investment amount. It was being held at a local restaurant that for that time period was closed to the public.

It lasted approximately six hours. During that time, we learned all we could about alcohol, the effects on the body, how impacts pregnant women, and the differences between premium, mid, and house liquors. We learned recipes, and the tools needed to either have a successful shift or bartend an event. This class was a lot of fun. I appreciated the fact that it was a mixture of people who were completely new to bartending, as well as ladies who had some bartending experience. Shout out to the *Bar Baddies*.

At the end of the class, we were given a quiz and we all did well. The final test of the day, would be that every one of us had to make a cocktail of our choosing. We were able to choose from the recipe list that they gave us, and get our first practice of being behind the bar. The very first cocktail I made was a *Sex on the Beach*. everyone loved it.

Here's the recipe if you're ever interested in making it at home.

Sex on the Beach

Fill a tall glass with ice
1.5 oz Vodka
1 oz Peach Schnapps
2 oz orange juice
2 oz cranberry juice

Sitting next to me in the class was a bartender who had been working in the industry for about two years. We instantly connected, (I never meet a stranger), and she told me that her manager was looking for another bartender to have on staff. I reiterated that this was my first ever bartending class and that I had no prior experience. Knowing this, she still believed that I would be a good fit for the job, and said that if I was interested, she was willing to train me.

I texted Jay during the class and asked his opinion, and he said that if I felt comfortable to go for it. After all, me gaining this experience would get us one step closer to our goal of moving to Las Vegas. I told her yes; I would be interested. She contacted her manager to let her know and then shared with me her information, so that I could call and set up an interview.

We received our certificates of completion that day, but there was also one final step – to take our certification exam for the state of South Carolina. This was an online examination, sponsored by SERVSafe®. I took my class within the week, passed with an 85%, received my certificate electronically, and printed a copy for my records.

That following Monday, I reached out to Ashley, the General Manager, to set up an interview with her. My interview was scheduled for Thursday of the same week. I walked in, met her, and we had a great conversation. Before, I left, I had the job! I couldn't wait to call Jay and

Emerald and let them know. I started my first bartending job that following Monday, and as promised Sweet Tee, the bartender who sat next to me, was there to train me. She worked with me for two weeks behind the bar, before giving me space to take the training wheels off.

While I had been on the job bartending, our plans for Jay's birthday trip changed. Since we were moving to Las Vegas, he chose that as the place for his 40th birthday trip. Emerald found a great Airbnb for us, with a pool.

None of us had ever been to Las Vegas, so this would be an all-around fun experience. Our flight was a little over four hours, which meant we would arrive in Vegas at about 10:30 pm PST. The flight was pretty smooth. This was my first time flying to the West Coast, so it was pretty exciting.

As soon as we got off the plane, we knew we weren't in Kansas anymore. Immediately I saw nothing but slot machines. There were so many people gambling that night. I had never seen anything like that before. Once we got outside of the airport into the Passenger Pick-Up area, I smelled nothing but weed. These were true "welcome to Vegas," moments.

The first thing we did was grab an Uber to get to our hotel. The airport wasn't that far away, so we didn't have a long commute. We arrived 15 minutes later. Check in didn't take long, so we were all able to get settled pretty quickly. We put the kids to bed. Everyone was tired. After all it had been a long day, but we weren't too tired to hit The Strip. After the day we had, we needed a drink. We found a daiquiri spot. I don't exactly remember what flavor I had, but it was good. It was just what we needed, nice and cool for a hot Vegas night.

The next morning, they went out to get the rental car, and once they came back, it was on and poppin!' It was time for us to go and explore Las Vegas. Prior to our leaving Columbia, they made connections with a realtor, so that while we were in Vegas, we were also able to do some house hunting.

This trip really solidified it for us. We did some touristy things, such as walk the Las Vegas Strip, and took Sydney & JJ to the M&M museum. We enjoyed ourselves just as much. Outside of the Las Vegas Strip, we were able to experience the "city of Las Vegas." Life outside of what we perceived it to be or saw on television or in the movies.

Las Vegas is a beautiful city. I thought because it was the desert that it would be flat land, lots of heat, and bone dry. Boy was I wrong! There were beautiful mountains all around with perfect indentations and plenty of red rock. I instantly said, *"Boy, you couldn't pay for these views,"* even though we really were.

I had a really good time and ate some great food, including trying some new restaurants while I was there. There was plenty of celebration, including a special birthday video that Sydney coordinated for Jay. This brought him to tears. During the trip, I even had an opportunity to meet Emerald's brother, sister-in-law, and niece, and nephew. They drove in from California to spend some time with us.

The Saturday prior to our leaving, Emerald's brother met us at Seven Magic Mountain and took photos of us. We were all dressed in our "Larry Boy," gear, a part of Jay's House Washington fashion label. By the end of the week, I could really see myself living here. The next day we left Las Vegas for Columbia. I would have to report back to work on that Monday, so this was plenty of time to get back in sync with the Eastern Time Zone. Trust me, if you've never flown to the West Coast, jet lag is real.

After being in Vegas for that week, we came back and turned up the heat on our moving plans. We started watching YouTube videos and following Las Vegas influencers on social media. Jay started having conversations with people who had been in Vegas at one point or another for business to get a feel for the climate out here.

At this point, the school systems were returning back to normal, and children were being enrolled back into school. We planned a celebration for the one-year anniversary of the I Won't Starve Academy, Jay's non-profit that he started during the Pandemic. I watched him make this celebration about the community he served and the people who had been instrumental in his life and I Won't Stave the brand. He chose this moment not to honor himself, but to honor those individuals who had poured into him as well. One of those individuals was me.

Lord, they got me on this day. I thought to myself, how in the world could I be helping to plan an event and have no idea about this. I appreciated this more than they knew. I haven't really been a person that's received a lot of "honors." While I appreciated the thought, it was weird for me to accept. I am happy being a member of the team. Jay and Emerald were becoming very special to me, and this gesture is only one example that truly speaks to their heart.

CHAPTER 13

Viva Las Vegas

After coming off of the I Won't Starve Academy celebration, which was amazing. I told you guys that I was shocked to receive an award. I've done this work with Jay over the last couple of years, and to me it was my job, no special recognition was needed. However, I am grateful that they thought to include me amongst those they were highlighting that day.

The time had also come for me to let my apartment go. This was bittersweet. This represented me keeping my word to myself and never making a late rent payment, my leasing office hated to see me go when I gave my notice. That never happened before. I have never experienced being in control of leaving an apartment under these circumstances. I was always forced to leave. However, once I told them I would be moving to Las Vegas in search of a better life, they were very happy for me. And I was happy and proud of myself for doing what I said I was going to do. As stated before, this was truly a year of firsts, and I was feeling more and more like this was my winning season.

I was no longer in a position where I had to borrow a car to get around to appointments and take meetings. Now, I had one. I had grown to having an office space inside of Jay's building where I could have clients meet me. Business was booming and it seemed as if everyone wanted to work with the Ink Pen Diva. I had made a name for myself, even taking on my first celebrity client out of Atlanta. Pinch me baby because I had to be dreaming.

Sydney had always expressed that she wanted to write a second book, and as we were approaching her birthday late July she brought this conversation back up. She reminded us that last year around this time we had gotten started on her first book. She thought it was a great idea for us to get started on this one. I agreed, and we immediately got to work.

We had to move quickly because Jay and Emerald came up with a great idea to take the family to

Universal Studios. The trip was going to happen in less than 30 days, so we had to get started, especially since we wanted to release the book at the beginning of October as in the previous year.

Immediately, Sydney and I moved into her next book, which would be named, *Malaysia's BIG Creation, Vol 2 of the Anti-Bullying Club Series.* Sydney was doing her usual cartwheels and flips, and I found myself chasing her around the house and the office to make sure she stayed on point. In the meantime, I was setting up a transfer from the Marriott in Columbia to the Marriott in Las Vegas. I found through my research that I would have to get all Nevada based licensing and certifications before I would have the opportunity to take the job.

At the beginning of August, Emerald and Jay were leaving for Malibu, CA to celebrate her birthday before going to Vegas to do some house hunting. I stayed in South Carolina to make sure business was still being take care of on the home front, as well as finishing up this book with Sydney.

I was doing a lot of work for J Haleem, LLC. At that time, Sydney was the only person I was working with as far as books were concerned, and that was okay because she needed all of my attention and we were on a tight deadline. Once Jay and Emerald left, I got a chance to have some amazing time hanging with the kids and of course working with

224

Sydney. But also, we ate like crazy. We did a lot of ordering out, including Chinese food and pizza, which we really enjoyed. I am sure Jay was upset because of all the money we were spending over the course of the week while they were gone.

Over the last few years, everything had become about work. There were way too many times that I could stand to count on my fingers and toes of me trying to figure out how I was going to make ends meet. Being able to go through this last year finally being able to take a breath, relax, and have fun was everything. This was a different experience for me.

We enjoyed the daily check-ins from Emerald and Jay while they were in Malibu. We heard all about the weather and good time they both were having celebrating before they headed to Vegas to get to work and try and find a house.

A couple of weeks after they got back, the time had come for us to take our trip to Orlando. This was planned in a manner that would allow us all to take one final family trip before the kids were going back to school. Universal Studios was a blast. Again, another first. It was great to see the kids excited about their experience and having fun, in a family atmosphere. It seemed as if they were having the time of their life, and as an adult I was too. It was nice to let our hair down literally before making this big move to Vegas. It was a perfect way to get us prepared for what was about to happen.

Meanwhile, I had to plan for me to go to Vegas, not too soon after we got back. Our conversations were not only heating up, but things were moving along quickly. While in Vegas, I had to take care of some bartending business to make sure I would be fully licensed and have all of my credentials. This would also be my first time flying by myself, and I was looking forward to it.

Working with Jay's Publicist, who was based out of LA, I was made aware of an opportunity for him in Long Beach, CA. He was invited to present the I Won't Starve Entrepreneur Development Workshop to the people of that city. This was a BIG DEAL! I learned throughout our time of working together that Jay thrives when he is able to present in person and he would have that opportunity in California. In the midst of everything else we had going on, we also added this to our calendar.

Always generous with his platform, he asked me to speak, and share a motivational message. Also on the platform was Naida Rutherford, one of the original speakers for Jay's I Won't Starve Entrepreneur Development Workshop. In Long Beach, he wanted to use people that he knew could not only deliver, but that had been with him on this journey. We planned this event over the next few weeks and made our flight plans.

This was another first, I had never been to LA before, so I was really looking forward to it. Jay LOVES California and it would be great to experience the city through his eyes. We arrived in California on a Thursday. Our first stop off of the plane was Randy's Doughnuts. Chile! When you walk up to the window, it's like Doughnut Heaven. Every flavor, topping, and style you could ever imagine. We ordered glaze and some other types, and my eyes lit up when I saw the red velvet. After all, I'm a Southern girl, and we love some red velvet cake. I chose not to get it and went with a glazed instead.

We couldn't wait to open that box of doughnuts. I had heard so much about Randy's from Emerald, from their most recent trip to California so, I was eager to try them. There was also a small bag accompanying the box. She got me the red velvet doughnut! She knew that I wanted it and surprised me with it. When it comes to good food, Randy's was just the beginning.

We stayed at a beautiful hotel downtown LA around the corner from the then, Staples Center where the Lakers play. The next morning, we went for breakfast at Mel's Diner on Melrose. Prior to our getting there, Jay went on and on about Mel's, more specifically the freshly squeezed orange juice. Of course, this had to be the first thing I tasted. Baby, after I took one sip – I pulled out my phone and did a reel about it on Instagram. To this day, it is one of my most watched! Mel's was great for the orange juice and old school diner feel, but Blue Jam Café, was DELICIOUS! That chicken sausage & egg scramble was to die for. Blue Jam was also fun because

Emerald's brother and her niece and nephew also came to visit us. It was so good to see them again!

After breakfast, we immediately had to get to work. Jay had to head to San Diego to meet with the staff and co-workers for the company he was consulting with. San Diego was about two hours away from LA. We rode down the Pacific Coast Highway and saw nothing but miles & miles of ocean. This was such a great experience for me. I saw him in his element. This company was on the ball. We met everyone in the office that day, and they even took us to lunch before getting back to the office and wrapping up some last minute details. It was then that he found out that we would be responsible for training all of the Southern California businesses that came through their company. What a great opportunity for our company and a great way to start the day off business wise. We left San Diego a few hours later, with only a few minutes to spare before we had to prepare to attend a Meet and Greet that evening.

Next up was The I Won't Starve Entrepreneur Long Beach. It was all that! We definitely made an impact on the people of the city. Jay was able to help out minority businesses in their government contracting endeavors. While he was wowing the crowd, I hung in the back with his Publicist to coordinate final details for his book-signing at Malik Books, in the famous Fox Hills Mall in Los Angeles. Jay hung around to sign books and take photos, but your girl was tired. It had already been a long day, and it still wasn't over.

Everybody who was somebody in LA held a book-signing at Malik Books, and we were honored to be there. This book-signing was an incredible success. We weren't sure what to expect but wound up having a great turnout. Jay has quite the network of friends in LA, and several of them came to the mall to not only see him but buy books as well. People were walking in to see what all the fuss was about. We were truly having a great time. Malik and I stayed close, and he let me know that he wanted to interview Jay on his podcast before we left for the day. I made sure Jay carved out time to complete this before we left the store that day. I even took it one step further and convinced them to purchase some copies to place on their shelves. This was a great day indeed.

Prior to going to Long Beach, we had received approval for a place in Vegas. Once we got back to Columbia, it was time for us to really get down to business. At this point, Sydney's second book *Malaysia's BIG Creation* was released. We foregoed the formal book release celebration because of everything we had going on and instead chose to enjoy a nice dinner with a few of her close friends and family.

November 8th is the day we planned to leave Columbia. The highway route was already mapped out. Jay and I would take the road trip together. Sydney and JJ were in school, and Emerald needed to stay behind with them. We would drive from Columbia to Atlanta. Spend the night in Atlanta, get up the next morning and drive to Oklahoma City, OK. From Oklahoma City, the next stop would be Flagstaff, AZ, and from there, we would make our way to Las Vegas. Every city stop was a 12-hour marker in our travels.

I spent the next couple of days, going to visit my friends and family around Columbia. This was my last "See you later," until I would make my way back to South Carolina. I started with my mom, sister, and nephews. The last person for me to visit with was my son, Dj. Dj had grown so much. He had a great job and was doing well in his own apartment that he had now completely furnished. I spent a few hours with him. I let him know how proud I was of him and his growth. I would certainly miss him most.

One of the hardest see you laters was to Emerald, Sydney, and JJ. We had grown so close over the last two years, spending time together and sharing special memories. Now, I would no longer see them every day and in fact, I would not see them again until the Christmas break. It wasn't only hard for me; this was hard for Jay as well. If you know him, then you know that nothing means more to than being a husband and father. To leave them behind was painful, albeit necessary in order for us to get settled.

We spent the better part of November 8th packing up. Jay and I would make the cross country drive in my car. We put as much of our clothing and personal items as we could in the trunk and in the backseat. This would be a three-day road trip and we needed to be prepared in all cases. If you've never had an opportunity to drive west or drive cross country, I encourage you to do so.

It was an amazing experience. The country is so beautiful. As you head out west, you start to see different changes in the scenery, buildings, and ways that people live. It was breathtaking. And I made sure to take lots of videos and pictures so that I could document our stops and our travels. This was the biggest life-altering moment for me. And I wanted to capture every one.

Over those three days that Jay and I were on the road, we became even closer. I told you guys that we connected over music when we had our first interview. We grabbed his CD case, yes, he still has one of those, and kept a nice rotation of good music playing and good conversation going.

Whenever we got really deep into our conversations and thoughts, we would call or FaceTime Emerald, so that she could be right there with us on the road. God was gracious to us during those three days. We experienced no car trouble. We saw no accidents but be careful driving through those mountains. Team J Haleem was heading west, and we were ready to conquer all that Vegas had in store for us.

I had never lived anywhere else outside of Columbia, so to make this move to Las Vegas was such a big deal for me personally. I remember Jay asking me, what this move would mean and for a long time, I started to get down on myself because I didn't seem to have a "deep enough" reason to want to move as compared to theirs. What I had to reconcile for me was my why. My why for moving could be found in several reasons, but the main one was because I needed a new start, in a fresh space.

While South Carolina is my home it also very much represented trauma for me. It was the place where I experienced incest, molestation, and physical and sexual abuse. Overtime, I believed this played into my mindset as an adult and my psyche and why I found myself in the situations that I chose to place in this book. I have learned that sometimes, you really do have to physically move and get away.

We finally arrived in Las Vegas on November the 11th. We started seeing more and more signs for Las Vegas as we got closer. The moment I saw the sign that said *City of Las Vegas*, I broke down and cried. Finally, we made it and I'm not only talking about the journey over those three days, but I'm also talking about from the moment this idea came into his mind.

He looked over at me and saw me crying. He asked if I was okay, and I was. I was. Silently, I prayed and thanked God for allowing us to make it, for giving us traveling grace, covering, and protecting us. I thanked God for what we had been working so hard for, for the last several months to finally allow this dream to become reality.

Tamika's Final Thought

At the time this book is being written, I have been in Vegas for almost one year and my bartending has becoming another business, *The Snatch Bar*. I am back full-time working and being the Ink Pen Diva and devoting myself to continuing to help authors all over the world share their stories.

At this point, we are all officially in Las Vegas as an entire team. Sydney and JJ are enrolled in school. Jay opened our J Haleem, LLC office, which is approximately 10 minutes away from the Strip and Emerald is doing well in her new job. I saw him put a master plan into place, working it every step of the way, with our full support and betting on him, and it worked. We made it.

As I bring this book to a close, I pray a few things over your life. One, that you allow what you have read to permeate your heart. Don't just take this as words on a page, or the sharing of my story – take it as a lesson, use it as a blueprint for your own private journey. Whether you choose entrepreneurship or not, life is not easy. It will be filled with many highs & lows, as you can see from my experience. Don't be afraid of the hard times, embrace them. It is what makes us human. I pray the greatest of God's blessings over your life.

From my heart to yours, thank you for taking this ride with me. Thank you for allowing me space in your heart to share a little more of mine. I pray that you fully embrace your truth, and that as you find strength, that you too will one day have the courage to share it.

Sincerely Yours,
The Ink Pen Diva

About the Author

What doesn't kill you makes you stronger is the motto of the five-time Author, Book Coach, and Publishing, Tamika L. Sims. Through years of opposition, domestic violence, and life's challenges Tamika has a story to tell.

As a book coach, Tamika's mission is to empower others to share their story with the world equipped with accountability, self-awareness, and guided instruction. Over the last eight years, Tamika has helped more than 200 men, women, and children, tell their stories, producing bestselling and award-winning books worldwide.

For over five years, Tamika served as a lecturer at the University of South Carolina – Columbia, where her debut novel, *The Plus Factor* was used as a required text in the Department of Women and Gender Studies. She has served as an expert in the areas of domestic and sexual violence for numerous NBC, FOX, and CBS affiliates.

Made in the USA
Middletown, DE
21 October 2022